A: le

Lisbane Press

To Susan who prodded
and Oskar who typed.

Published by Lisbane Press

Printed by Belfast Litho Printers Limited

1

When you have lived the allotted three score years and ten, you find you have accumulated a great number of memories and stories which your family have heard over and over again, but about which recently they have begun to say:

"Mum, before you go, please write them down". And so it is in response to this request that I now set pen to paper.

I suppose I had better begin at the beginning. I was born in 1914 into a moderately well-off family. My mother at the time had whooping cough, caught from my eight-year-old brother, and so, at the age of half an hour, I was whisked off to my grandmother's. She lived on the Malone Road, we lived at Knock, a district not considered as posh as the Malone Road, but nevertheless a pleasant suburb about three miles from the centre of Belfast. These early travels and the supposed changes in the milk of the two districts were later blamed for my peculiar tummy upsets, and early on I was labelled "delicate". It made me feel inadequate, a failure somehow, and I grew up longing to be as tough as everybody else. However, I was kept at home with a governess until I was nine, having substituted my sick turns for fairly regular bouts of bronchitis.

Castlehill Road was still a country road, quite unbuilt on, when with my governess I took our afternoon walk along it. Quite often we met a uniformed nanny in charge of a little girl of my age coming from the opposite direction. They had a magnificent Newfoundland dog, we had Jack, a not very well bred Fox Terrier, who was getting old. Our two warders acknowledged each other's presence with a polite inclination of the head as we passed, the other little girl looked eagerly at me, but I had eyes for nothing but their beautiful dog. Old Jack decided a wide detour was the better part of valour. These encounters continued until one day we met in Miss Nairn's dancing class, at which point our warders decided they might speak to each other and names were exchanged. The other little girl was Monica Allen and she lived in

Stormont Castle; she was an only child and her mother was anxious for her to have some friends of her own age. I, too, was virtually an only child, because my brother was away at his boarding school. So I was invited to come to tea with them after dancing and later I was delivered home regally in a Rolls Royce!

The Allens were Christian Scientists and I don't know if it is general among Christian Scientists, but there were some things they did not want Monica to know. When the lovely Newfoundland ate poison and died, she was just told he had gone away and I was told not to tell her he was dead. If anyone had told me our old Jack had gone away, I would have wanted to know where he had gone and when he would be back, but Monica seemed to accept this and fortunately did not question me. And one day at dinner in the nursery (I was now invited to spend whole days with the Allens) her governess, who had by now replaced Nanny, asked me if I would like some rhubarb. I said: "I am sorry, the doctor doesn't allow me rhubarb". "Who is the doctor?" said Monica. I cannot remember what answer the governess gave. I was overcome to find I had blundered into something else Monica was not supposed to know about.

My mother, in return for all the hospitality I had received, invited Monica and her governess to tea with us and suggested that the governess should have tea downstairs with her and the children as a special treat could have theirs in the nursery. My nursery compared in no way with Monica's. Hers had the biggest rocking horse I had ever seen, almost as big as a real pony, and although I should really have grown out of such things, I spent many happy hours imagining myself galloping over the countryside. She also had a Teddy Bear bigger than she was. However she took a friendly interest in my play things. The room in the front of the house had a wide three-sectional window and at first we opened the window and danced my dolls on the sill, then we let them tap on the centre pane, then we climbed out and took them to the further pane, then a lady came up the drive and enquired of our maid if we were aware that two young children were out on the window sill; then Monica was seized by her governess and hauled inside. I was scolded, of course, although I don't think I had started this performance, and always afterwards Mrs. Allen said to my mother "But you won't let them be by themselves". My mother was a little sceptical about Mrs. Allen's faith. Monica's nursery had bars on the windows.

Sometime when I see on television politicians being welcomed to Stormont I chuckle to think that they will never enjoy the fun we had rolling down the very steep banks in front of the castle. One day, when we were sitting in a heap at the bottom, we saw a funeral passing on its way to Dundonald cemetery.

In those days funerals were horse-drawn and the black horses often had black plumes nodding on their heads.

"What's all that?" asked Monica.

"It's a funeral".

"What's a funeral?"

"What they do when they bury people".

"*Bury* people?"

"Yes. I mean when they're dead, of course", and then I remembered I should not have said that. But I could not have left her thinking they buried people alive.

When I was seven, we went on holiday in Scotland and I remember my father reading out of the paper that Stormont Castle had been sold, it was to become the residence for N. Ireland's own Prime Minister and that a building for our own parliament would be built on adjacent land. I was thunderstruck. What would become of Monica? "She will be all right", said my father, "it says here Mr. Allen has retired from the shipyard and is going to live in England". And the lovely rocking horse?

When we came home, the Allens had already left and when, a few days after the auction at Stormont Castle, I saw the summer house, where we had so often played "house", mounted on a carrier's cart, jolting and shuddering through Knockdene Park on its way to its new home, I felt my life had really come to an end. Certainly I have never since been returned home in a chauffeur-driven Rolls Royce.

The firm of Atkinson & Boyd had offices on the second floor in Bedford Street, when King George V and Queen Mary came to Belfast to sign the agreement separating the Six Counties from the Irish Free State, by which it was hoped peace would be established after that period of troubles. This was done in the City Hall, and afterwards there was to be a procession along Bedford Street and back by Gt. Victoria Street. We had to be in our place very early and then for hours nothing happened.

One lady, possibly hoping to alleviate the boredom, said: "I expect we have to wait for the Queen to powder her nose", almost a naughty suggestion which occasioned much laughter among the grown-ups. I looked at her doubtfully. My notion of royalty had largely been derived from Alice in Wonderland; I remember I had a painting book in which

The Red Queen had a truly horrible face. I could not imagine why she should want to powder her nose or what good it would do her, if she did.

When the procession at last passed beneath us, from our aerial viewpoint not much could be seen of King George under his plumbed hat, except his knees and his boots; and I could not imagine the stately lady beside him screaming "Off with her head" at anybody. Altogether my first glimpse of royalty was mystifying, but I thought all the horses were wonderful, and was outraged when told that "the rebels", as we called then, had bombed the train taking them back to their barracks on the Curragh.

2

Usually we went to the sea each summer, living in rented houses at Ballywilliam outside Donaghadee for two months. Nowadays people with cars commute from there to Belfast, but in those days we had no car and the removal was really quite an undertaking. Although only eighteen miles away, Donaghadee seemed like a far distant place and the packing-up for our visit was extraordinary. So far as I can remember we had to bring our own linen and cutlery, but then there were so many things that our cook was sure we would never be able to get in Donaghadee that I think she would like to have brought all our pots and pans if my mother had let her. When all was assembled, a carrier came for the baggage and Billy McNarry from Donaghadee came for us. No bus linked Ballywilliam to Donaghadee and so every morning Billy collected my father and my uncle and others and drove them to the train which then puffed its way to Newtownards, meandered around Scrabo to Comber and thence through Dundonald to Belfast. And in the evening he met the train and drove them back. My father quite often managed a swim before breakfast and a round of golf after supper in the evening; and sometimes, to my great delight, he engaged one of the fishermen to take us out fishing between the Copeland Islands.

He took his holidays normally around the "twelfth week" in July, not that he took any interest in the Orange rallies. They were something that concerned our domestic help. With the rented houses went the services of a man, who cut the grass, raked the gravel and ran the engine which pumped the water, and when he took his two days off for "the 12th" and the maids also disappeared to watch the processions we were left on our own. Our cook had left us well supplied with cold food, so there was no problem there, but with the water there was. For some reason we were not entrusted to run the engine and so it had to be pumped by hand. I can remember how we all took turns to wind the big wheel. I thought it was great fun and was rather sorry when the man came back again.At first the houses had oil lamps and candles, but later some had their own electricity, and the engine which pumped the water also charged the electricity.

The holiday in Scotland, where we learned that Stormont Castle had been sold, had not been entirely successful. I had started to be sick before we even left home, and the following year in London after three days of intensive sightseeing I went to bed with bronchitis. I remember my brother's utter disgust "She's not ill again, is she?". So my mother thought it easier to cope with her puny wee waif in a house of our own where you can be sure of the food, or the water, or the milk or whatever it was that was supposed to have upset my tummy, and the funny thing was that nothing in Ballywilliam ever did. So my poor father was heard to say: "Well, here we are again. The same rocks. The same old seagulls". It may not have been his idea of an adventurous holiday, but I wished for nothing better.

I was aware that the seashore at Ballywilliam did not fit the picture of the seaside in children's comics. There the children were always digging sand castles against a background of tumbling breakers and imposing cliffs. Our shore was stony with outcrops of rocks and the waves made a crisp little "church" sound as they broke and then rattled the pebbles as they drew back. Sand there was in patches here and there, and instead of cliffs a stout sea wall, which was just as good for climbing.

Children nowadays wear much more sensible clothes, shorts and jeans, but those were unheard of for girls in my young days. My mother engaged a sewing woman every spring to make my cotton frocks and then, fearing that it might be chilly for my bare legs when we went fishing in the evening, she got the woman to make me a pair of grey flannel bloomers to be worn under my dress! I cannot imagine what it must have looked like, yet those ghastly bloomers were the one garment I made sure was not left behind when packing up for Donaghadee.

Having no car and only an occasional char-a-banc (more of them anon), catering might have been difficult for my mother, had it not been for the number of traders who came round selling on the doorstep. I well remember Jinny the Fowl woman. Her dress reached her ankles and was completely enveloped in a starched white apron over which she wore a cardigan whose pockets sagged. On her feet she wore men's boots, on her head she wore a hat known as a sailor hat, although I had never seen sailors wear such a thing; it was of shiny black straw, turned up all round and secured with two murderous hat pins. And on each arm she carried an enormous basket full of chickens beautifully plucked, trussed with a wooden skewer, their giblets tucked into their wings as you never get them nowadays and each basket covered with a snowy white tea cloth. Somehow she also carried a large umbrella. She came from somewhere about Six Road Ends, took the train and then started to walk out from Donaghadee, selling as she went. Her first port of call was Miss Glass's boarding house on the outskirts of the town, where she probably lightened her load considerably, and so he continued until she reached Ballywilliam, two miles further on. "Now there's a fine pair of birds for you, ma'am. Three shillin' each I'm askin', but I'll give you the pair for five", and she would beam a smile at me.

Herrings arrived more spectacularly. It was like a chariot race between two rival fishmongers with the ponies going at full gallop and the boys standing up on the flat cart shouting "Herrin's alive, herrin's alive, Ardglass herrin's". If anyone signalled that they wanted some, the poor pony would be reined back on its haunches, the boy would jump down, degut the herrings with a speed that had to be seen to be believed and then, as his rival had now got ahead, would be off again at full gallop. Later in the day they would be seen straggling back to Donaghadee, the carts empty and the ponies frequently lame.

When I was eleven, my father got his wish about going somewhere different and we had a holiday in Cornwall, and although there were golden sands and cliffs and Atlantic breakers, it wasn't the same. Something was missing.

So, for a few more years we went to Donaghadee. By then I was riding a bicycle and was allowed to go off on my own as and when I pleased. My mother had had a serious operation when I was five and for many years had been a semi-invalid, advised to take things easy. She spent most afternoons in a deck chair in a sheltered corner of the garden, if she could find one - my nurse had earlier described Donaghadee as "the coldest place on God's earth. There's not one bit of shelter you could put a pram out in".

When I think of the appalling things that happen to little girls on their own nowadays I am surprised that I was allowed such freedom. The traffic, of course, was negligible, but I was warned to be careful going up to Orlock Hill. This became a sinister place for me. It was dark, overhung with trees and the road rose sharply to twist round a corner. I half expected one of the monster char-a-bancs to come down on top of me. They were enormous vehicles, their seats arranged athwart their body and high above the wheels, each "pew" having its own door. They were open to the elements, but put up a canvas hood when it rained and could only be entered by climbing up the treble running boards. When they had a conductor, he would collect the fares by shuffling along the top running board and leaning into the "pew". Otherwise you paid the driver, when you had managed to get him to stop.

I had discovered a man living in an old railway carriage on the far side of Orlock Hill who kept kennels which I thought was an ideal occupation, and so despite the terrors of Orlock Hill and the char-a-bancs my mother found a note (prophetic perhaps?) on the hall table "Have gone to the dogs".

I was passing through a fiercely "pro-animal" phase and used to infuriate our cook by going round the house snapping the mousetraps in case they caught one. I must have been a perfect little pest. My uncle had given me a well-bred foxterrier pup, but I was angry, because it had had its tail docked. My uncle was my mother's eldest brother and very much the head of her family; it was explained to me that he knew about horses and dogs and that you could not have a foxterrier with a long tail. I did not see why. I was told to say thank you nicely and stop being silly. I loved my Peter dearly, but ever since I have never had a dog with a docked tail. I prefer tails as God made them and usually find them amongst the mongrels. And then, one day I went with my mother through the old Smithfield Market and saw a shop where they sold larks in cages. How could anyone expect a lark to sing, if they kept it in a cage?

When asked what I wanted for my tenth birthday, I said, "Money".

"What for?"

"I want to buy larks."

"Whatever for?"

"To let them go."

My family considered this.

"The cats will only get them", said my brother.

Nevertheless, my parents thought I might be indulged to the extent of ten shillings ("if we give you more it may only encourage the trade") and Morris was dispatched to Smithfield.

He came home with two. One, which the man said had recently come in, cost 7/6, but the other had been in some time and he would let it go for 2/6.

I took them both into our back garden and let out the older one first. It half flew, half scuttled into the bushes and the cats may have got it, but at least it had a chance, and I still remember the feeling I had as I saw the other soar away over Knock Bowling Green out towards the open country.

3

"I do hope you won't be too far behind the others", said my mother when it was decided to send me to school, "we've maybe kept you at home too long". This did little to remove my inferiority complex.

The school I was sent to had only twelve pupils. My mother thought there would be less risk of infection in a small group. It was run by two sisters, former governesses, in their own home , but it disappointed me. It had no desks or blackboards like they had in the comics. Instead, we sat in two carpeted rooms, separated by sliding doors, round large tables, six at each. Looking back now, I realise how fortunate we were. We got individual attention and no one was allowed to pass on until everyone had got there, be it long division or weights and measures or 1066.

On my first morning it was explained that a card would be given at the end of the week to the pupil with the highest marks, and at the end of the year a prize to the one with the most cards. I looked round at my school fellows and thought how bright and confident they all looked and how nice it must be for them to be given the cards. But at the end of the week the card was given to me.

"To you?" said my brother, "Are the others not all back from their holidays yet?"

And the next week the same thing happened. After which a curious idea entered my head, so curious that I determined not to tell anyone about it until I had that prize safely in my school bag. Which was what I did.

After two years in my little school I went to Richmond Lodge which by modern standards would also have been considered a little school. That was in Miss Purvis's day. Competition for prizes was discouraged; instead, through the Dalton System of Education a kind of carrot to the donkey led you on to do extra work. Certain compulsory work was set each week which had to be done before you began the optional work, which was more interesting. As it often took the form of illustrating what had been read, and as I liked drawing and was reasonably good at it, I enjoyed my time in Richmond Lodge very much. You learned to work on your own and teach yourself, which I think is the most valuable thing your education can do for you.

However, at that time it was thought necessary to be sent to boarding school; many from Richmond Lodge went to St. Leonard's in St. Andrew's in Scotland, but I, together with about half a dozen others, went to Folkestone. My mother had heard that St Andrew's could be cold in winter and thought the climate in the South of England would be better. My first winter there, 1928, was the coldest the South of England had had since records began, I think. Everything froze, the water in our tooth jugs and even a section of the central heating pipes. However, I survived and eventually grew out of my bronchitis.

The church in Folkestone was High Church. Accustomed to the rather austere simplicity of St. Columba's at Knock, at first I felt like a fish out of water. Little acolytes in scarlet cassocks and short white surplices lighting candles on the communion table, which was always called the altar, a robed all-male choir being proceeded by a large cross held high, all this was very strange indeed to the eyes of a fourteen-year old Protestant from N. Ireland. Then the school asked for the names of those who wished to be confirmed, I wrote home that I would much rather be confirmed at home, but my parents replied that would not be possible, I would never be at home to attend the classes. So I gave my name in.

Gradually I became aware that the congregation was much more reverent than at home, there was a greater sense of worship. When exhorted "Let us pray", there was no one who did not kneel down properly - something which sadly is not nowadays very much observed in the Church of Ireland. And the vicar did not preach. He gave a short informal talk from the pulpit, easily understood by us schoolgirls. And every Sunday I looked forward to the anthem so beautifully sung, with the choirboys' angelic trebles soaring up into the roof, completely dispelling my doubts into thin air. I was not just confirmed, I was hooked.

The vicar took the confirmation classes himself in the same informal way. He was Canon W.H.Elliott and later when he moved to a parish in London, he became well-known on the wireless as "the Thursday night man". Long after I left school I frequently listened to his words on Thursday nights.

I found my new school full of irritating and petty restrictions which were inhibiting because you soon learned to keep your head down and your mouth shut. I might have regretted my time in England, had it not been for two things: one was the mistress who taught English Literature and who read aloud so beautifully, and the other the friendship I made with Molly Clutton-Brock. She invited me to her home in Oxted for the half-term weekends, and later I spent many happy visits to their cottage at Mullion in Cornwall, in fact Molly's home became almost my second home in England. To most Irish people England is a place seen through the hotel window, but thanks to the kindness of Molly's family I felt I had got inside and felt at home there.

My father had rather old-fashioned ideas about girls earning their keep. It was the time of the depression and he felt it wrong that girls should take jobs unless they had to. My mother, too, looked forward to having me at home, but they weren't going to have me sitting around doing nothing. So I was sent to the College of Art, then housed in Belfast's Tech., where I took some classes, but did not enlist on a full diploma course. A dilettante, I'm afraid, but happy to be so. I don't think I should have liked to become a teacher or a commercial artist.

4

One year after we had left school Molly wrote to say that her family were sending her for six months to a family in Frankfurt-am-Main and couldn't I come too? Although I did not know a word of German, I jumped at the chance. My father ascertained that I could attend art classes in the Stadel Institute and off I went.

That was the winter of 1932-33 which might be called the last winter of Germany's freedom. The Nazis were there, mostly miserable little men in ill-fitting uniforms, jangling collecting-boxes at the street corner, their fingers blue with cold. No one paid much attention to them, they were not yet in the driving seat. The family we lived with did not like them, but like so many others in Germany considered politics a dirty business, all right for those who liked that sort of thing, but pointless for ordinary people to become involved, an attitude which proved disastrous, for it simply made Hitler possible. However, these things did not concern us either at that time.

Along with other foreigners, mostly Indians and Japanese, we went to classes in the university which taught German to foreigners. From there we joined the Foreigners' Club which organised trips to places of interest and sometimes dances. I suppose it was Molly who said I could draw when the organiser wanted a poster painted. When I brought it to him, he kept on repeating *Ausgezeichnet*. Now I knew that *zeichnen* was to draw, but I could not see how a poster depicting two gaily coloured Chinese lanterns swaying in the breeze with a flurry of confetti and streamers could possibly be "out of drawing". There was no perspective in it. From his manner he was pleased and thanked me profusely, but I went home and looked up that word, just to make sure. My poster was not "out of drawing" - on the contrary.

My Christmas in Germany was something I shall always remember. On Christmas Eve we went with the family to the Römerberg in the old centre of Frankfurt and entering the church filed past what I thought was a rather gaudy representation of the Crib. Maybe it only seemed so to Protestant eyes. Outside, the square (it is not a very square square) was packed with booths selling everything imaginable from hot sausages to special Christmas confections and little presents. A band was playing carols and people were singing. Then we went home, but were not allowed into the living room until all was ready. And then the sliding doors were rolled back and there stood the Christmas tree in all the glory of its newly-lit candles. No German child is supposed to know of the existence of the tree, much less allowed to see one, until this magic moment on Christmas Eve.

They sang a carol and we all went in. Little tables for each person had been ranged round the room with, beside their presents, a plate of traditional Christmas baking, which seemed to me a much more orderly way of doing things than our custom of grovelling about under the tree. Christmas Eve was an intimate family gathering, but Christmas Day brought together a much wider collection of relations.

Fasching, the period before Lent, is the occasion for festivals with people in fancy dress dancing through the streets from one party to the next, certainly in the Rhineland and most other Roman Catholic parts of Germany. The foreign students were asked to do something for our *Kostüm Fest*, for which I had done the posters. There were four Scottish men at the university, one Scots girl, one half-Polish Scot and the two of us, and we decided we would do an eightsome reel. We rehearsed rigorously, the men sent home for their kilts and created quite a sensation when they appeared on stage in them. I was doing my solo bit in the middle when I noticed the others were trying not to laugh. I hoped I was not the cause. It was only after the curtain came down that I learned one of the men had lost his pants! He had felt them slipping and gone skippity-hoppity into the wings, kicked them off and returned to his place in the reel, apparently unnoticed by the audience who may have thought it was all part of the dance. Anyway, it proved they do wear them.

Hitler was increasing his rallies and his torchlight processions, but we never went to any of them, not even when he came to Frankfurt. We made the excuse that he bawled so much you could not hear what he said. Instead, a party of us went down to Mainz for the carnival on *Rosen Montag* and enjoyed ourselves. But one of the floats depicted the League of Nations as a very sick patient. I felt hurt. Miss Purvis had brought us up to believe it to be the hope of the future, and I had not realised there were people who ridiculed it. At eighteen, I suppose, I was naive.

We managed to join the Students' Skiing Club. For about £10 you could have a fortnight's holiday in Bavaria with skiing instruction and railfare included. The railfare was 3rd class, of course, not the most comfortable, hard wooden seats, but we took it in turns to stretch out on the luggage racks. The men lived in a youth hostel and the girls were billeted three or four to a room in houses in the village. It was dark when we eventually arrived and thankfully tumbled into our beds. Next morning the beauty of the landscape took my breath away. The surrounding mountains glittering in the clear sharp air, the brilliant sunlight on the snow-clad village, the thick snow on the roofs of the houses, sitting like marzipan on a Christmas cake; and over all a great silence and a feeling of peace. In those days there were no chattering ski-lifts, no pistes for lunatics to go hurtling down, the only sounds were an occasional sleigh bell as a small horse drew a sleigh piled high with hay to some distant shed. The milkman on skis with an enormous churn on his back slid, with a faint hiss, into the village street. It all seemed unreal like a theatrical set, and when the breeze disturbed the powder snow on the pine trees and the air filled with rainbow tinsels, it was magical. It seemed a pity to spoil the untrodden snow with our tracks and our "sitzmarks" as we beginners floundered about.

But on that fateful Sunday in March 1933 all the German students had to go down the valley to vote. I do not know if it was compulsory, but there were very few people out on the slopes that day. And when the result was known, some students were jubilant and one of them shouted something, which I did not catch, at a girl whose name was Neumann. She turned quickly and went into the house. I did not now then that Neumann was a Jewish name. I only wondered why she was in tears.

When we got back to Frankfurt the next batch of skiers met us at the station. "Everything is changed", they said, "they sacked so many professors, the university had to close for several days. And now the Nazis stand at the door and challenge everybody who wants to go in. They challenged Callum who said, "I'm not a Jew. I'm a Scotsman", at which we all laughed and said, "What is the difference?". We were shamefully light-hearted.

5

My mother had not been in good health for a number of years and was delighted to have me at home. She wanted me to take over the running of the house, although with two well-trained maids who had been with us for years I thought it was well able to run itself. However, I tried to busy myself with domestic affairs and became chauffeuse-companion to my mother. I enjoyed myself as I think many young women of my age did at that time. We went to dances and tennis parties and involved ourselves in charitable good works. I seemed to get roped in as a waitress at every fete that there was, but few of us had paid jobs. In fact, I remember my father being quite critical of a friend of his who allowed his daughter to become a hospital almoner "because she did not need the money". My father gave a great deal of his time for free to the interests of the Children's Hospital, and he expected young women to do the same. It was long before the days of the Welfare State, when welfare, such as it was, rested heavily on voluntary effort.

In Richmond Lodge Miss Purvis had so often talked about our having an obligation to the Community, of the need to do something for those who were not as fortunate as we were, so in 1928 the old girls of R.L., the Arellians, set up the first Nursery School in Ireland. They were an indefatigable band of pioneers who not only raised the money to build the school, but kept up the pressure to get it recognised by the Education Authority. The superintendent and her assistant, both Arellians, were fully trained, but the rest of the scheme depended on a rota of volunteers, drawn from the Arellians, as cooks and helpers. In 1933 I joined the rota of helpers.

I also went to a riding school fairly regularly. When a pageant of St. Patrick was going to be performed in Belfast Castle grounds in 1934 the organisers asked the riding school for ten horses and riders. As I financed my riding out of my dress allowance, a day in the saddle for free was not to be sniffed at. Also, the libretto, if that is what you call it for pageants, had been written by Richard Rowley who was married to my mother's cousin, and I was interested to see what he had done - also for free.

So, on a glorious summer's day we trotted two by two along Sandy Row, accompanied by excited children, and up the Antrim Road. "Oh dear me", said a hot and harassed young curate when we arrived, "we had no idea the Roman soldiers were going to be ladies". "Four of us are" we said. "Never mind", he said cheerfully and, diving into the men's changing tent, returned with an armful of costumes and accoutrements for us. I thought it prudent to select a helmet in golden papiermache, which fitted me relatively well and, most important, had a chinstrap, but by the time I had done that the only sandals left were one which fitted me and one which was an outsize man's. Well, so long as I don't come off the horse and have to walk, I thought. Meantime the only helmet left for the riding instructress was one that someone had sat on. It pinched each side of her head and had a rocking movement. She, having walked the course, so to speak, the night before, was the only one of us who knew what we were supposed to do.

Eventually we mounted. We were encumbered in our right hands with a spear whose shaft was so thick it did not allow our right hand to do anything more than grasp it. Our left arms were burdened with a plywood shield whose raw, unrasped edge jabbed uncomfortably on our bare knees. We had beautiful golden hockey pads protecting our shins, but that is not where the stirrup leathers nip you; it is much higher up.

However, we trotted into the arena with due decorum. There we had rather a long wait whilst our centurion bid farewell to the little British village and the boy Patrick, leaving them to be overrun by the marauding Irish. We were supposed to represent the Roman withdrawal from Britain. The day was hot, the flies bothersome, the horses restive, two of them who had once been raced were very much on their toes, doubtless stimulated by the presence of the large audience. But when at last our centurion had finished his farewells, he mounted his horse and at the head of his troop trotted across the stage and swung out of sight behind a mercifully large rhododendron bush. At which moment there came a tremendous burst of applause and all the horses, with one accord, bolted. Most of us managed to pull up when we reached the main avenue at the top of the hill, leaving behind a trail like a retreat from battle, shields and spears having been cast aside in our effort to control the horses, but the two former race horses continued at full gallop right down to the front gate, where they encountered some late-comers trying to come in. The horses swerved abruptly and both riders fell off, which must have startled the late-comers, especially as the riders were quite badly damaged by the gravel of the avenue.

Meantime our instructress was supposed to turn back and attempt to drive off the Irish invaders, and she certainly scared them for real, because her helmet descended like a candle snuffer and she was unable to see where she was going. The audience seemed unaware of these happenings.

Later in the drama we had to appear from different parts of the woods as four Celtic kings, representing the four provinces of Ireland, each followed by a groom. Mercifully we were divested of our Roman accoutrements and I had managed to find two sandals that I could walk in. Our kings dismounted and went to hear St.Patrick's sermon and we girls held the horses. It as even hotter by now, again the flies were bothersome and the horses were beginning to feel they had just about had enough. Eventually the kings returned and we dutifully helped them mount and then got up ourselves, but one groom's horse played up and refused to stand. They circled each other until her king dismounted, put his groom up and then got up himself. But again 1 never met anyone in the audience who noticed. Maybe they too, like the German audience in Frankfurt, thought it was part of the performance.

6

I spent the next few years doing this and that. Molly and I with some of her cousins went to Oberammergau in 1934. Nazi flags floated from every house. After the performance we moved to Garmisch-Partenkirchen, but it was terribly crowded. Dollfuss had just been murdered and the Austrian frontier was closed to Germans, but not to us, so we moved up to Seefeld, a very pleasant little village with a small lake, the whole area bereft of tourists, which was bliss.

Coming down from a wonderful walk in the mountains one evening, I thought I would have a quick swim before supper. Two women with their children were sitting on the shore. They looked up at me in some surprise

"Fräulein", they said, *"est ist elf Grad."*

"Ja", I said and smiled.

"Mademoiselle, il fait onze", more urgently.

"0ui" I said and plunged in.

When I looked back they were hurriedly gathering their children together and departing, not wishing to remain in the presence of a lunatic.

When I got back to the hotel I asked the others what temperature the water is at home. None of us knew. "What did it feel like?" they asked. "Refreshing", I said. Now, of course, that we have been introduced to centigrade temperatures on the weather charts I realise that llC is quite chilly, and no native would dream of putting a toe in before 20C. But that could not possibly be "refreshing".

I also began to get interested in sailing. Hitherto the peace of Strangford Lough had only been disturbed by the River Class, raced by the nobility and gentry who lived round the shores. On alternate Saturdays their races were started by Major Blackiston-Houston's butler with a shot gun on Calf Is1and, and by a member of Lord Bangor's household, similarly armed, at Audley's Roads. The rest of the craft consisted of a few sailing and motor boats from which people caught mackerel or went out for picnics on the islands. But about this time it was decided to start an inexpensive class of racing dinghies for young people and the class chosen was the International Snipe Class. At once, the nobility and gentry rose in alarm. Strangford with its ferocious tides was no place for small capsizable dinghies, especially if sailed by inexperienced youngsters. Their concern may have been a very laudable one for our safety, but I had a sneaking suspicion that they sensed that should sailing for other classes become popular the serenity of Strangford would be gone and the lordly uniqueness of the River Class's racing would be no more.

Nevertheless, in spite of a certain amount of adverse criticism, a class of some twenty-five boats came into being and moored itself in Whiterock Bay, then almost empty of boats. A small wooden hut was erected on shore to act as a clubhouse.

At first I was only concerned as a crew, but as all the owners were very keen on collecting their points and wanted to have their boats raced for them when they went on holiday, and as I, by some fluke, had done rather well, I was never short of employment.

I remember my very first regatta. It was not even called a regatta. It was called the Quoile Aquatic Sports, which was probably more accurate, and was held at the old quay far above where the barrage is now. The "Sports" included greasy pole, swimming and rowing races as well as a race for Snipes, which involved beating up through the Cut, only about twenty feet wide, so that much frenzied cross tacking was employed. There were also several natural hazards, such as mud banks, reed beds and irate swans. A loudspeaker on the quayside blared out pop music of the day "Little Sir Echo, how do you do? Yoohoo, Yoohoo", the sun beamed down and spectators and competitors alike enjoyed that summer afternoon in lovely surroundings.

Regattas were also held in Strangford, Portaferry and Kircubbin, ending in Whiterock. They came to be known as the Strangford Week. These involved not only the Rivers and the Snipes, but almost any craft, that could raise a sail,on a handicap basis. There were even two ancient fishing boats "to be raced as fished", that is, they were not allowed to discard their gear and hoist a lot of extra sails. The races at Strangford and Portaferry started on the incoming tide, described a wide triangle in the southern end of Strangford Lough and then, the tide having turned, came skimming back to the finish on the ebb. This left a slack period when all the boats had disappeared into the Lough and the organisers sought to fill the gap by having the Snipes scurry backwards and forwards across the raging tide. Ronald went ashore to remonstrate that this would be extremely dangerous. He was told that there was nothing to entertain the holiday crowds, until the boats came back, to which he replied he did not intend to be the sacrifice for a Roman Holiday. He was stiffly told that Portaferry Regatta was not a Roman Holiday - that was at Cook Street.

Nevertheless he prevailed on them to let the Snipes sail the same course as the other boats, and none of us entertained the crowds by drowning.

Lord Bangor and his daughters entered into all the fun and games after the race was over. As we gobbled our meal below in "Sarita's" cabin, we heard his Lordship, who at that time was Speaker of the House at Stormont, trying in his most authoritative tones to get a rowing race started.

"Come along now, I want you all in a straight line".

"Come on, you chaps, get into line. Blue boat, do you hear me?"

"Now look here, you chaps, I'm not going to start you, until you get into line. Blue boat, will you please come back".

Then another voice broke in: "Hi, Jimmy, will you take yer bloody boat away to hell outa that". After which the race started without more ado. Which goes to show that it is not what you say, but the way you say it.

After the race had started, there came a sprittle over the water, as of sudden rain, which reminded us that his Lordship's butler was still using live shot, and we hoped that the provocation of the blue boat would not tempt him to cease pointing it heavenward.

When all the combinations of rowers had been exhausted, single oarsmen, pairs with two oars each, pairs with one oar each (these were the ones that caused the collisions, because one partner pulled harder than the other and they were unable to steer straight; they disengaged by blattering each other with the oars and sometimes continued on shore), as I said when all these diversions were over, we strolled up to a field outside the village for the land sports. There were the three-legged, the sack and the obstacle races. I remember a dog which ran out just as the cycle race approached the bend and the look of astonishment on its face at the havoc it had caused.

I found myself roped in for a ladies' race and made immediately aware that the young women of Strangford run not only with their feet, but employ elbows as well, quite viciously. I quickly drew out of the scrimmage by running round its outer edge which gave me a clearer view of the course. Like the Quoile, it also had its natural hazards, nettles, thistles, ragwort and cowpats, but having a clear view I was able to weave my way between these blemishes and romped home ahead of the field.

The evening had turned damp and chilly, and many of us were wearing oilskins, some even seaboots, when the loudspeaker announced that the next race would be for yacht people "to be run as sailed" (like the fishing boats). In view of Lord Bangor's white hair and short legs, he was allowed to start half way down the field, ladies about a quarter and the rest of the rabble behind. Seaboots are difficult to run in; there comes a time when they begin to run you and steering is no longer possible. However, we maintained these social, sexual and athletic distinctions until about ten yards short of the finish, when I think someone tripped and all creeds and classes came together in a sprawling tumult of oilskins which, when it picked itself up , was found to have poor little Lord Bangor as its bottom layer. Somehow I think regattas are not what they used to be.

And the next day, as we slid out of Strangford harbour to cross over to Portaferry, a voice on the wall above said: "Sammy, look at here. Thonder's the gairl that can run", but in case you think my ego was becoming too inflated, I was brought sharply down to earth a few days later in Kircubbin: as I walked up from the harbour, only touching the ground in spots, having just won a race, another voice assailed me: "Hi. missus, yer boat's away. The rope she was tied till was tied till nothin'."

7

In order to keep up my German I had joined the German circle, a group who had mostly been to Germany to study music. We had only one real live German, Rudolf, who was very crushing in his corrections of our grammar and pronunciations. We used to meet about once a month, the first part of the evening being given to reading some book or play and then, after tea, it dissolved into someone performing lieder, which sometimes was a merciful release. Round about Christmas 1938 I missed one of the meetings and my friend Peggy told me afterwards: "You missed something the other night. A new fellow's come from Germany, chap called Rudnitzky, and he contradicted Rudolf flat".

I said: "Lead me to him". However, when I eventually met the new arrival, I thought him so good-looking he must expect all the girls to chase him, and so, to show that I was not a chaser, I cocked my nose in the air and went my way. He just thought I was a rather snooty English type. It was nearly four years later when we married.

Oskar as I first knew him.

8

1938 was the year my mother died and my brother joined the Territorials after the Munich crisis. In the spring of 1939 my father had a slight heart attack. The doctor recommended rest and a complete change, possibly a cruise. My father refused to go anywhere near the Mediterranean. With Hitler announcing periodically that he had no further territorial claims in Europe and then occupying somewhere else, my father said if we went into the Mediterranean we would never get out again. It was Nancy, my sister-in-law, who suggested that we took one of the slower boats going to the Argentine and visit my uncle Henry, my father's brother, who worked with the Argentine railways in Buenos Aires and who would be retiring in a few years' time. So off we went. It took about three weeks, stopping for a day in Lisbon, Pernambuco, Rio de Janeiro and Montevideo. Devoid of the wealthy Brazilians, who only travelled on the fast boats, the company on board was very agreeable and small enough in number to be able to get to know nearly everyone, before we reached Buenos Aires. There was one rather imposing gentleman, whose name I have forgotten, but for whom Lloyd-Noyes might be apt, who kept strolling up to people and asking: "Do you come out often? I come out twice a year to visit my estancia, you know, La Paloma in Enter Rios." Eventually I asked someone: "What's so special about Enter Rios? Why does he always mention that?" They said: "That's *the* place to have an estancia. There are very few left in private hands, they've nearly all been bought up by Bovril or United Canneries".

I do not know if since our recent disagreements there are still newspapers printed in English in the Argentine, but in 1939 there were two. Although the text was in English, the photographers and the type-setters had no knowledge of the language. There was a story that they once printed a picture of a prizefighter in training for his next fight and one of the Pope blessing the faithful, but they got the captions crossed. However, it was the custom of the reporters to meet the ships as they arrived and scan the passenger list. We arrived after dark and as we came down the gangway were startled by a number of flashes. Next morning there we were under the heading: "ON HOLIDAY FROM EUROPE. Mr. Atkinson and his daughter on a visit to their estancia La Paloma in Enter Rios, pictured here with friends who met them on arrival - that was how my uncle and aunt were dismissed. "I'd like to see old Lloyd-Noyes' face when he reads that", said my father. On the whole, I thought I would not like to be anywhere about on that occasion. So began a very pleasant visit with all my uncle's friends exclaiming: "You never told us your brother had an estancia".

Passing Harrods one day, my father saw a very attractive looking box of assorted sweets in the window and thought he would give it to my aunt, but although the shop is a branch of the London firm, not all of its employees, like those of the newspapers, speak English. The girl brightly showed us a little boat made of meringue, in which ice-cream or fruit might be served at a posh dinner party. "No", said my father, "I want a box of sweets. SWEETS". The girl conferred with a colleague. Together they dived under the counter and hopped up on ladders, alternatively registering perplexity and sudden inspiration, until a most astonishing array of confections was assembled, log cabins, castles, ships, even something like the Taj Mahal studded with cherries and angelica. To all of this my father was saying ever more loudly "I just want a box of sweets". Other shoppers were stopping to look. Finally the manager, when summoned, said: "We send for Miss O'Hara", at which my father's face lightened considerably. I think he thought dry land was in sight. But it fell equally quickly, when round the corner came a sleek and soignee young negress in a pink Elizabeth Arden overall. She advanced towards us, waggling everything she had got, listened attentively with her head cocked slightly to one side and then with one flash of her magnificent teeth said: "Aw, you mean kendies!". "In our country" said my father, "we call them sweets", just so as she would get it right for next time.

When we came home we found everyone very edgy, living from one newsbroadcast to the next, some were digging air raid shelters in their back gardens, others were scoffing at the idea that there would be a war, so that when war was declared in September of that year, it came almost as a relief. At least something was settled, ghastly though the thought of it was. I well remember that Sunday morning the third of September. My father and I were getting ready for church, but we waited to hear Mr. Chamberlain's announcement. There was an extremely loud thunderstorm over Belfast at the time, almost as if the war had already started, and I watched the raindrops creeping down the window pane. I felt they were a portent of the tears to come.

Morris was called up and with the 8th Anti-Aircraft Regiment was sent to Cornwall for training. As they marched into York Street station,

Dad and I were on the pavement to see them pass. After they had gone, my father blew his nose and then remained very silent as we drove away. I would quite like to have joined up too, but now I felt that my place would be at home with him.

That first year of the war became known as the “phoney war”, nothing much happened, but everyone was busy preparing for what might happen. I went to First Aid classes and A.R.P. classes, we grew more vegetables in the garden and I bottled fruit, whilst there was still sugar. I kept up my art classes and my day in the Nursery School.

Then, after Dunkirk, when invasion seemed imminent, the evacuation order came into force. Contingency plans had been made for the Nursery School to go to a holiday home for girls in Carnlough, but they had not been very well thought out. The place was not ready for small under-fives, who need a great many pegs and hangers that they can reach and no one had really considered how long voluntary helpers with home commitments can be expected to continue working as volunteers. Anyhow, we descended on Carnlough with sixty children, two trained teachers and ten voluntary helpers.

It had been intended that at peak periods - getting the children up and dressed in the mornings and putting them to bed at night - all twelve of us should look after a ‘family’ of five, but at other times only half of us would be necessary and the other half could have time off. But we found that we had to spend our time off screwing in hooks, putting up shelves and finding boxes to keep toys and equipment in. One or two of the children had been known to have lice from time to time, but in those first few days we had all been too busy to look, and when we did look we found the lice were rampant everywhere, in fact one helper even found them in her knitting.

So I appointed myself Louse-Officer-in-Chief and set up my barber’s shop in the back garden. There, in my time off, I happily snipped away, the shorn locks were wafted off in the breeze and clung for days on some rather scraggy old rose bushes, and then I set in with Lysol and a fine comb and combed and combed. Years afterwards, when I trimmed my own children’s hair, other mothers would ask “but how did you learn?” “Just something I picked up in the war”, I said.

After some weeks I went home for a couple of days’ leave. My father, looking at my finger tips, said: “Is that nicotine?” I think he would have been less shocked, if it had been.

Carnlough was not really a very wise choice. Had bombs been

falling on Belfast, it might have been a good place to be, but not if invasion was the real danger. We were disconcerted a few days after we arrived to find soldiers putting up barbed wire between us and the beach. It was near enough Belfast for the mothers to come down to see their children, and so children, who had been happily settled, as soon as they saw their mothers again wanted to go home. Every weekend there were painful scenes. And so, with numbers dwindling, we approached the Home Office and they took over those children, whose mothers really wanted to have them evacuated, and settled them in Co Tyrone on a more business-like basis, no longer dependent on voluntary help.

I applied for a job in the censorship and was very pleased when I was accepted. At last I was actually going to be paid for doing something - £3/5/0 a week I think it was - and I remember, such was Belfast's attitude to women working, that there were actually irate letters in the press stating that jobs in the censorship were being given to ladles who did not need the money.

I wonder if Florence Nightingale's nurses were paid; many of them were "ladies". However, I utilised my unladylike standing by blowing my first week's pay on a dress I bought in Goorwich's for exactly £3. You could do that in those days. It was a very nice dress, too, and much admired.

After a week's training I felt like a fully fledged spy catcher, but that was as near as I ever got to catching one. Instead, we had to plough through piles of ill-written, unpunctuated scrawls, which said little more than that the sender was well and hoped the recipient was too. Sometimes he says he is enclosing "the usual", but does not, and that gives a lot of bother. It has to be verified that "the usual" was not in the letter when the censor opened it. The ordinary reader does not cut bits out, but has to refer to the head of the table who does the cutting - mostly references to weather conditions which might have grounded our aircraft and therefore have been of interest to the Luftwaffe. A snowfall and fog in England had us queuing up to be excised. I do not think that I am releasing any state secrets when I say that there was a list of doubtful organisations, whose activities should be watched, and many such styled themselves "British". One day my neighbours were fussing together over a letter and one went up to the head. When she came back, she said: "Would you believe it, they're cows!. At which I sat up and said: "What are?" "The British Friesian Society". They were quite annoyed with me when I laughed so heartily.

The Belfast Committee for German Refugees had been formed in the spring of 1939 when I was away with my father, but I had since helped giving English lessons, and discovered incidentally what a difficult language it is to teach; the pronunciation seems to have neither rhyme nor reason. My friend Peggy was an active member on the Committee and when the secretary left to get married in 1941, she suggested that I should join her as joint secretary. I thought that I would rather deal with people than read dull letters and so I left the Censor's office.

Belfast was bombed in April 1941 and again at the beginning of May. We had frequently had alarms before and so, when the sirens went, we thought it was just another alarm. But we soon began to hear a peculiar knocking sound, as if someone was sweeping with a wooden brush and knocking the skirting-board, and then some louder bangs. Not taking it seriously, my father and I foolishly stood watching it all at the hall window. Flares were being dropped which made the night as bright as day; we were amazed to see the shadow of our house thrown up on the house opposite; a tremendous fireworks display of tracer bullets was rising up from the docks, where we later learned there happened to be an aircraft-carrier in for repairs, but by far our worst nerve-shatterer was the battery behind us at Dundonald. Their first round went off with deafening parade-ground efficiency: one-two-three-four; their second round: one, two, then three and later four; their third: one, two .... a pause .... then three, and then, when you had at last taken your fingers out of your ears - four.

However, when we saw what had happened to the Antrim Road that night, we took the next raids more seriously. We moved the maid with her bedding out of her attic bedroom and put her under the kitchen table, and then my father and I tried to squeeze under the stairs and soften the contours of the gas meter with cushions. We were very cramped, nevertheless my father managed to nod over and started to snore, at which I crawled out and, as there seemed to be a lull in the bangs, went back upstairs to bed. To lose sleep for bombs was bad enough, but for snores was the limit.

After that it was decided that Knockdene Park should prepare itself for war. Most of the residents were of my parents' generation, but amongst the few younger ones Freddie and I underwent a firefighting exercise. After crawling through a smoke-filled tunnel, we emerged, somewhat grubby, to be awarded with a tin hat each (to Freddie was given a whistle, but as he suffered from chronic asthma I doubted if he could be relied upon to have enough breath to blow it) and an arm-band each saying "Leading Fireman", which would have been most impressive, had we ever had any firemen to lead. Instead, we persuaded the neighbourhood to band itself into three-man stirrup-pump teams, of which my elderly aunt's team, consisting of herself, her companion and her maid, were typical. The houses were of different sizes and shapes, being the product of individual Edwardian builders, with pitched roofs and dormer windows, where incendiaries might nestle. Freddie suggested we needed a good ladder, but was told that if he went to the scrap yard there was plenty of wood going cheap, and was advised to make one. He came away muttering that although he was prepared to do many things for his country, to break his neck off a rickety ladder was not one of them.

So we relied on our stirrup-pump teams, and fortunately the Luftwaffe never came back.

9

The Refugee Committee was an ecumenical gathering, but predominantly composed of Methodists and Quakers. The Methodists had given a room in Grosvernor Hall without charge, the Committee, whose funds were limited, had rented a 'phone and from one of the refugees a typewriter. The Committee met once a week and were very conscientious in visiting and reporting on where help was needed

I should explain to those who never knew or who may have forgotten, the conditions under which refugees were admitted to this country. They had to prove that they had a job to go to, that they were not displacing a local applicant for the job and that they would not be a burden on the tax payer. Queen's offered some places to students whose studies had been interrupted, some schools offered free places to younger people; some generous individuals laid down £50 to guarantee the maintenance of some young person. However, there were many thousands inside Germany who wished to go to America, but who had to wait for their quota number to turn up. In the last few months before the outbreak of the war it was obvious that these quotas would not be reached in time and, largely due to the pressure being put upon it by Victor Gollancz and others, the British Government issued transit visas so that refugees could wait for their quota numbers in this country, provided the Refugee Committees accepted responsibility for their maintenance. I am glad to say that the committees all over the United Kingdom and in both parts of Ireland responded magnificently. And then the war broke out, all possibility of emigration to America ceased and the committees, whose resources were limited, found themselves facing the possibility of maintaining hundreds of refugees for the duration of the war. Once again the Government was approached and once again the answer was humane: if refugees could find themselves jobs, they should be granted permits to work.

Most of the women had no difficulty in finding jobs as domestic servants or dressmakers, but with the men it was more difficult; only one or two dentists or doctors, who were very highly qualified, were allowed to practice, but the numerous lawyers were told they would have to re-qualify in the laws of this country. All had to appear before a tribunal whose purpose was to sort out possible enemy agents from innocent refugees, a task which I very much doubt could ever have been achieved by a process of questioning in a public court. However, by some rule of thumb they were graded into three groups. The A group were to be interned straightaway. The B were doubtful, largely because they still had a male relative in Germany who had not managed to escape, and the Cs were above suspicion, but all were subject to restrictions: to be at home by 10 p.m., to apply for permission to change their address, they were forbidden to enter the restricted zone (within ten miles of the coast) and to possess a camera or a bicycle. Many a time subsequently I wondered if these restrictions ever hindered a real Nazi agent or only those who were prepared to obey them. The refugees, having first-hand experience of the Gestapo, obeyed them implicitly.

And then, after Dunkirk in 1940 when invasion seemed imminent, the order came to intern all category B people. The men were first sent to a camp near Liverpool and later to the Isle of Man. The women were taken to Armagh Jail, where in a matter of weeks their cases were reviewed and they were all released.

The men could be released if they volunteered for the Pioneer Corps, and this a certain Dr. Berliner did. He was a middle-aged lawyer who successfully passed the required security screening, but then failed the medical test because of diabetes. However, having been cleared on security, he was entitled to be released, but before that happened the camp in Liverpool was bombed, some of the inmates were sent to

Scotland, others to the Isle of Man, and what became of the papers authorising Dr. Berliner's release no one ever discovered. So the whole process began again after much correspondence from us. Again he passed on security, again he failed the medical, but still the camp authorities seemed incapable of putting him on the boat to Belfast.

His wife and mother-in-law tried to make ends meet by taking a lodger, but when in April 1941 Belfast was bombed, the house was slightly damaged, the lodger fled and the firm which had been keeping a place for Dr. Berliner evacuated to the safety of Tyrone.

One Friday morning when I was alone in the office, Lola and her mother came in. They were so decent, so patient, so polite. "We know it doesn't do to bother the authorities too often, but do you think you could write another letter? You see, there is so much to decide. should we try to get the house fixed and find another lodger? What should we say to the firm that are keeping the job for Fritz?"

"Yes," I thought after they had gone, something has got to be done and I pulled over the typewriter. More in sorrow than in anger I wrote a politely restrained letter, setting out the facts and emphasising how so much depended on getting Dr. Berliner here. I concluded by urging the camp commandant to move heaven and earth to get Dr. Berliner on the boat to Belfast, but then some little imp that sometimes visits me hopped on the typewriter and I added: "but should these remain immovable, would you please try raising hell".

When I reached the office on Monday, Peggy was already reading the carbon copy. "Darling", she said, "what have you been writing here?"

"About time they got a letter like that".

"But don't you realise the camp commandant is probably some peppery old colonel exhumed out of retirement?"

In that moment I saw him: bushy white eyebrows and moustache's bristling with indignation as he turned purple up the back of his neck

"Oh dear", I said, "do you think I've got Dr. Berliner interned for the duration?"

"M'm", said Peggy non-committally.

The office was not very large and I spent the rest of the day shuffling round Peggy, trying not to meet her eyes. Tuesday was spent in much the same way, but on Wednesday there on the table lay a telegram advising us to expect Berliner off the Liverpool boat on Thursday.

"Well, you got away with it this time", said Peggy.

I know that as you go through life trying to do what you can about its messes and muddles you should not look for gratitude, yet when people do say thank-you, it is very rewarding.

And there on Friday morning were both the Berliners. "We wanted to show you, he really is here", said Lola, "and we both want to thank you for all you did for us. All the letters you wrote". As the door closed behind them, Peggy said: "Little did they know, poor dears".

Here, on this happy note, this tale might have ended, but there was a little post-script. The following spring a conference of all the Refugee Committees was held in Birmingham. Peggy and I attended and, having amassed all the permits necessary to set foot on the other side, we were not going to waste the opportunity by coming straight home. Peggy had three sisters, not seen since the war began, and I wanted to visit my friend Molly to see what she had married. So we went down to London and Peggy thought we might also call in at Bloomsbury House, the headquarters of all the refugee organisations, both Quaker and Jewish, to discuss some of our problems. Accordingly she made an appointment to see Miss Ruth Fellner, one of the high-ups, and as we were ushered into her office, Peggy turned and said: "And this is Miss Atkinson, my colleague from Belfast".

"Not Honor Atkinson?" said Miss Fellner.

"Yes", I said, wondering how she knew me.

"I read a letter of yours the other day", she said, extending her hand.

"I've just got back from a tour of the internment camps on the Isle of Man".

Here I was aware that Peggy's little toe was depressing my little toe. She had a knowing smile on her face which suggested "here it comes now".

"Yes", continued Miss Fellner, "you know the camp commandant was tickled pink with that letter you sent him. He has it pinned up on his door and shows it to all his visitors."

All I can say is that that peppery old colonel, if such he was, was exhumed from retirement with his sense of humour intact. Mercifully.

The Committee, as I have said, was composed mostly of Methodists and Quakers with a few other assorted creeds or possibly none, who wanted to help. What I like about the Quakers is the way they accept people as they are instead of fuming about how awful they are. Some of the refugees were difficult. One lady, who had once sung in the chorus in Vienna, seemed to think that this entitled her to the airs and graces of a prima donna and as a result was very difficult to place in a domestic job. She wanted to have her fifteen year old daughter with her, which made it even more difficult. At last Canon L'Estrange found amongst his parishioners two old ladles who wanted a cook-housekeeper. They lived in a large house on the Malone Road, which had a housekeeper's sitting room which seemed ideal, the child would not always have to live in the kitchen. But when the mother went for her interview, she raised so many objections at sight of the large kitchen range - "but who will carry the coals for me?" - that the old ladies decided she would not suit.

At the next Committee meeting Canon L'Estrange was very annoyed and suggested we should let her stew in her own juice and find a job herself. But the Quaker ladies just said: "Yes, we know she's tiresome, but we must consider the child's future" and went on to discuss connections they had who might be written to in England.

Canon L'Estrange looked across the table at Dr. Hickey, our Roman Catholic member, and said: "Dr. Hickey, this is no place for us. These people are angels".

Most of the refugee children quickly adjusted to life in their new country. They realised in a very grown-up way that they were on their own, that if they were going to make good, exams would have to be passed, and fortunately they were very successful in doing that. But there was one boy who posed a problem for the Committee. He was a likable, hearty type, an only son of elderly parents who had sent him at the age of twelve to a friend of his mother's in Belfast without ever explaining to him about the Nazis. Poor boy. It is hard to imagine how difficult it was for him to be sent, as he thought, on a holiday and then to find he was to live indefinitely in this foreign country, to go to school here and learn his lessons in English, a language he had only begun to learn. When the situation was explained to him, he said he often wondered why, when a knock came to the door, his father jumped into the wardrobe. He must have found it hard to accept as true what these strangers told him of his native land, when his parents had never mentioned such things.

However, he very sensibly decided to make the best of it; he tried very hard with his English and became quite fluent, though not perfect, but having failed Junior in all subjects but German, an academic career was not for him. It seemed that what he needed was some family life where in return for his keep he could do something useful. Somebody suggested "those people on the farm down at Portaferry who asked for a refugee student and we sent them Rudnitzky, perhaps they would take him". So Werner was sent to the Campbells.

But the lady in Belfast who had acted as his sponsor and who knew his parents thought he ought to be given some training to fit him for a job. Correspondence with the Campbells ensued, until I suggested that I should go down to discuss the matter. Petrol was rationed, but I got an allowance "for welfare" - four gallons a month I think it was - and I thought I would mix business with pleasure. I enquired of Oskar, who was going to be there over Easter, if there would be any chance of a horse to ride. He responded with enthusiasm and I and my young cousin spent an enjoyable day on the farm. We were warmly invited to come back and help with the harvest which we eventually did. It was arranged that Werner should do a course in book keeping and metal work at Portaferry Tech.

About this time Peggy went to do welfare work in England and I was left to manage the office on my own. I found myself answering queries on matters that had never previously crossed my mind: who, in rented accommodation, should supply the bulbs in the landing light or the toilet paper; who should brush down the stairs. I always pronounced in favour of the refugees, because I thought some landladies were trying to put things on to them.

Oskar began to drop into the office more frequently for no apparent reason except for a chat. One morning he arrived just as I was getting ready to remove our difficult prima donna, who repeatedly fell out with her landlady, to new digs. The Committee had previously footed the bill for her removals, until I suggested that as it was only about a hundred yards further along the Lisburn Road I could do it in my car. "After all", I said, "she can't have all that much stuff". Little did I know. So, when Oskar turned up I enlisted his help which he readily gave and we set off.

Unfortunately, the lady suffered from a defect common amongst refugees: she never threw anything away. Poor Oskar staggered down the stairs with packages and parcels, tennis rackets with broken strings and an empty bird cage.

"But you've no bird", I said.

"Some day I may have one", she said, "I so miss my little Mitzi".

So we packed it all into my car, drove it along the road and after we had stowed it into its new home, I said to Oskar: "I think you have earned a drink". His face brightened: "But you can't go into a pub", he said. His landlady was what was known as "good living" and had infected him with her views.

"Well, let's find a pub and we'll see", I said.

After that Oskar began to drop into the office even more frequently.

10

That summer my cousin and I returned to the farm in Portaferry. For the first time I tried milking a cow. None of the cows thought much of my efforts, in fact I think I lost more in sweat than they did in milk, and it was humiliating to find that Oskar was already an expert.

Here perhaps I ought to explain how it was that Oskar had become an expert farm labourer. Queen's offered free places to refugee students whose studies had been interrupted by Hitler, and although Oskar had already a law degree after four years' study at the universities of Berlin and Frankfurt am Main as well as one year as a practising lawyer, he was unable to make use of these qualifications in this country, and so he applied to Queen's to study for an Arts degree, and after his first year was granted a free place. Mr Fullerton, who was chairman of the Refugee Committee, was also chairman of the board of governors of Methodist College. Many of Methody's staff were married and disliked having to return to the school in the evenings to supervise the boarders' prep. and so it was arranged that, if Oskar undertook these duties, he could have free board and lodgings. It was a most satisfactory arrangement, because he could pursue his own studies whilst keeping an eye on the pupils.

This left him with only the holidays to be settled, and it was then that Philip Campbell, himself a Queen's graduate, offered a holiday job to a refugee student, and we sent Oskar. He turned out to be a most useful farm hand and from then on spent all his vacations on the farm.

The Refugee Office had always had very good relations with the Police. At the start of the war they had come to see us and said they knew there would be many wild rumours and statements made about our "flock" which they were bound to follow up, and we could help by advising our people not to talk German in public places and to obey all the regulations.

We ran one or two student "hops" for the younger refugees and Mr. Moffat, who was head of the Aliens' Department, came to these labelling himself "Gestapo", which fortunately was received with amusement. In that way he got to know many of them and form his own opinion. This was fortunate, because at about this time a debate was held at Queen's and it was reported to the police that a refugee had made a fervent pro-Hitler speech, but unfortunately the only refugee whose name the informant knew was Rudnitzky. Oskar was called in for an interview. He explained that he was not a member of Queen's debating society and had never attended any of their debates.

"I didn't think it sounded like you", said Mr. Moffat. "Just bring me a chit from the secretary saying you have never been there."

The Ministry of Labour became aware, possibly through another busybody, that Oskar was apparently teaching in Methody without a labour permit, and he was called to an interview at Stormont. The tea trolly was just passing and his interviewer bought him a cup before getting down to business; when all was satisfactorily explained, Oskar was enchanted. He simply could not imagine either of these interviews taking place in the Germany he had just left.

However, when internment was ordered, the police arrived on the farm to arrest Oskar. Philip Campbell, who was a J.P., stood firm and declared that he would testify on oath that Oskar was no spy and that he needed him on the farm. Oskar also protested that as a stateless alien he could not be an enemy alien. His father was Russian and although Oskar was born in Germany, under German law minors took their father's nationality. After the first world war his father became a naturalised German, but Hitler later annulled this and declared that those non-Aryans who had become naturalised were now stateless, and Oskar, who was then a minor, was stateless too and entered this country on a Nansen passport, designed for stateless persons.

The police withdrew whilst the matter was referred to the Home Office, and meantime Oskar was advised to stay on the farm and observe all the regulations that applied to enemy aliens.

So that was how Oskar, in the process of becoming a B.A., also became an expert farm hand. He had even mastered the technique of reversing the rick shifter up against the haystack. Nowadays farmers no longer make haystacks, which had to be shovelled up and carted off to the stackyard on a piece of equipment like a giant dustpan. I, having driven a car for about ten years, was well able to manage the tractor going forward, but reversing with the rick shifter behind me the most astonishing things happened. I actually missed the haystack. Patiently Oskar would explain reverse helm to me.

Philip ran the farm with the help of one active and able-bodied man, Alec, his old father Robert James, a sweet old man, and two other men of retiring age. In the evenings Oskar sometimes walked into Portaferry with some of the men for a jar, and on the way home Robert James, after he had had a couple, would start to sing. But as they neared the chapel, he would say: "Now hush, boys, hush". Reverently removing his cap, he almost tip-toed past the chapel, and once on the far side resumed singing again in his cracked old voice. His wife sometimes used to wander both in her mind and in her person, so that periodically the cry went up "She is away again", and all work stopped until the old lady had been rounded up and returned, if not to her right mind, at least to her own hearth-side. There never seemed to be a dull moment. There were bees which swarmed at inconvenient times, bullocks who broke out - mostly on a Sunday afternoon - and an attractive looking squadron of Muscovy ducks who flew overhead in a bee-line for the corn field. "Ruddy air mail ducks" Robert James called them.

By now Oskar had graduated and was waiting to start his first job teaching Latin in Regent House school. One lovely Sunday afternoon we walked up to the windmill above Portaferry, and as we sat looking down on that breathtaking view, the little town below, Strangford opposite with the silver swiftly flowing current gleaming between, the same idea occurred to both of us: it might be nice, if we got married. Nothing was said at the time, in fact, so far as I remember, we held a quite serious conversation about education. Nevertheless, an idea had been born.

When Oskar returned from his first day at school, he suggested that we should celebrate his first day in employment with a jar in Dummigan's. I cleaned myself up and slipped into a pair of slacks I had originally bought for my South American trip. In those days ladies wore slacks only in navy blue or grey flannel, but these were rusty red linen and a great success on the trip. Subsequently they were worn at on-shore parties after regattas and became known as my "Red Sails in the Sunset", a popular song at that time. They also created a stir in Dublin, when the Royal Irish Y.C. invited a team from the Strangford snipes to race them in their Wags. I had the impression, as I entered the dining room, that the whole place had stopped eating. Afterwards in the ladies' changing room I was besieged.

"We're so glad you did it."

"Did what?" I asked.

"Wore trousers in the dining room." I then noticed they were all wearing skirts. "We've always wanted to, but never dared."

Poor dears! But maybe that has all changed now.

And now, as we walked along the sea front, I noticed that some of the curtains in the cottages twitched as we passed.

When we came out of the pub, it was raining and so we arrived back very wet, but very, very happy. It was no longer just an idea.

11

About this time we acquired a very unusual maid. I could write a whole book under the title "Some maids I have known", but I shall restrain myself.

We engaged her through an agency in Co. Sligo, and her father wrote asking if she could be met as she had never been to Belfast and would not know her way about. Accordingly I was there in good time, expecting to meet some shy little country waif, but as the passengers left the platform, only an attractive young woman with an elegant bandbox on her arm was left. She stepped forward and politely enquired if I were Miss Atkinson and, finding that I was, said "I'm Elsie". So we set off together for Knock. I took a poor view of that bandbox which was the only luggage she had, my mother having once told me that you can tell how long the maid intends to stay by the luggage she brings.

However, Elsie settled in very well. She was a pretty girl with a gentle, agreeable manner, she spoke with a pleasant Irish accent, articulate and grammatically correct, the sort of girl you would engage to look after children. She had delicate hands and there was an air about her, the way she moved about and set a plate down on the table, which suggested she had not been reared in a bog. When we discussed the day's menu, she would consider my suggestions and then make her own, which were often sensible improvements. She knew about using things up, a great asset in wartime.

Several visitors remarked that she was no ordinary maid, and learning that she came from Eire said, "Obviously she's a spy". In fact, Freddie always referred to her as *"Olga Polowska"*. However, there seemed little she could spy about in our house and she seemed reluctant to go out by herself. I had pointed out the local cinema to her, but she said: "Some of those American films are so silly you wouldn't want to waste your time watching them". She seemed content to sit in the kitchen, sewing or knitting, which was also unusual.

And then one day a friend said: "Do you know what your Elsie told me this morning? She said she was going to Cairo for Christmas".

"She hasn't said anything to me", I said, "does she want to join the

ATS or what?"

My father and I discussed this information, but decided to ignore it.

Then about a fortnight later a tall, well-built figure in a raincoat, cycle clips and unmistakable R.U.C. boots appeared on the doorstep and wished to speak privately. He produced a telegram. It was addressed to King Farouk and stated: "Am willing to come. Please arrange detective escort" and was signed "Princess Faizelle, 18 Knockdene Park". I said I simply could not explain it, but assured him that I certainly had not sent it. However, I told him we had this maid, a perfectly satisfactory maid in every respect, who had made this odd remark about going to Cairo for Christmas. Perhaps it was some sort of joke.

"The Censorship doesn't take kindly to jokes of that kind - not in wartime", he said.

"I don't wonder", I said, thinking of how it must be buzzing.

"I think, maybe we'll make a few more enquiries", he said. He took her home address and departed.

Again about a fortnight later - looking back we noticed how there seemed to be developments at fortnightly intervals, possibly connected with phases of the moon - my father wakened me one morning to announce "Elsie is gone. She's left us this note".

It was a neatly written, correctly spelt and punctuated little letter, stating that she was sorry she had to leave us so suddenly, but we must understand she was a ward-in-chancery, and yesterday (her day off) she had met someone who advised her she must go at once to attend to affairs of state. She signed it Elsie, not the Princess this time.

We informed the police and her father.

Concerts were not plentiful in wartime, so the neighbourhood had formed a gramophone circle. We visited each other's houses and brought our favourite records. The circle was due to come to us that Saturday evening, and Oskar was coming for the weekend; we had not yet announced our engagement, although my father had given his consent.

In the middle of the gramophone recital the police in Ballyhackamore rang up to say they had Elsie. The Gardai had found her in Longford. I said:

"I can't cope with her just now. Could you keep her until morning?"

"No", they said, "We can't lock her up, she hasn't committed an offence".

"I'll go down and fetch her", said my father, and did so.

The gramophone circle's interest in music had dwindled by this time, and after they had left, we held a serious discussion. My menfolk simply dismissed the whole affair as the outcome of a vivid imagination, probably stimulated by romantic magazines or films.

"But she never went to the films", I said. "I don't relish being dependent on a girl whose imagination may cause her to flit the next time we are having a party".

Next morning a death-like silence filled the house. I lay doggo, wondering if she had already flown and how my men, who had been so confident the previous night, might propose to deal with the situation. However, in the end I decided that somebody had better feed the hens, and I got up.

After breakfast I went up to her room. She said she felt so exhausted after her travels that she did not want to get up. She stretched herself luxuriously, and I wondered if she were seeing me as a Nubian slave expected to bow out backwards. I told her to get up, and eventually she did.

During the next few days our kitchen heard the most fantastic tales and I sometimes came out of it wondering which of us was dotty, Elsie for spinning such fantasies or me for standing there with my mouth open lapping them up. She described with great clarity the ivy-covered gate lodge where she had stayed in Longford; the people who lived in it and who were kind to her; how the farmer in Sligo was not her father; she had been born in Egypt and he had stolen her and brought her up with his own children, but now he made attacks on her life; when they went riding, he put ropes across the road to trip the horse, and so on. I was getting bewildered.

We had written to her father asking him to come and fetch her home, emphasising that she must be seen by a doctor as she suffered from delusions. He replied that it would take time to get a permit to enter the North, but that if we put her on a train, he would meet her at the border. He regretted we had this bother with her, but he did not seem surprised, which made us think it might all have happened before. Maybe he was used to having Elsie returned wanting.

I knew one of the doctors in Purdysburn Mental Hospital and I rang her up and related this strange tale. She said: "Well, you may think she's perfectly normal except that she thinks she's an Egyptian princess, but without assessing her I would say she's an advanced case of paranoia-schizophrenia, and I advise you to get rid of her, because if she thinks her father makes attempts on her life and you are in touch with him, she may turn on you".

"Well, could you take her into Purdysburn?"

"If she is from Eire, she should not be on our rates".

Lovely. I began to peep behind the kitchen door whenever I went in.

Once more I sought help from the police. If we could just have a policewoman to go with her in case she jumped off the train, but no, that would only be possible if she were under arrest, and she had not committed an offence. So in the end we wired her father the time of the train on the day appointed. She very politely bid me good-bye, shook me by the hand and said we would read all about it in the paper when she raised her case in the House of Lords. Then she and my father went off in the waiting taxi.

We waited for a letter from her father. When it arrived, he thanked us for all we had done - which had not been much - and said she was now in Sligo Asylum. Poor dear. I hope that was the right place for her. He also asked what she had done with her clothes.

I went up to her room and found the most extraordinary collection of bits and pieces; sleeves cut out of some things, collars taken off others and made into little posies with bits of ribbon. I parcelled it all up and took it to Knock post office.

"Have you got a permit?" said Miss Anderson.

"What for? It's only old clothes".

"You can't send it into Eire without a permit".

"Well, how do I get a permit?"

"You will have to apply to the Board of Trade".

"But I'm not setting up a business in old clothes".

Nevertheless I applied and in due course they replied to say, if we could give an assurance that it would not occur again they could grant a permit.

My father said: "Let me answer that".

He wrote that it was unlikely that we should again have a maid from Eire, and if so, she would go off her head, and if so, she would leave her belongings behind, therefore he thought we could give the required assurance. And that really was the end of the story of the Egyptian princess.

But my father's interest had been aroused. She had several times mentioned the name of a family "in the big house", a name I have since forgotten, but my father looked them up and found that they had property both in Co. Longford and in Co. Sligo, and that a member of that family in the Diplomatic Corps had been in Egypt in the 1920s. His guess was that Elsie was this man's illegitimate daughter who had been reared by one of the tenants. With her refined features and gentle manner she probably was like a canary amongst the sparrows, and this had so preyed on her mind that the princess had been created.

A tragic story really.

12

Although the Committee had asked the Campbells to take the young boy Werner, Philip thought he would like some more help with the harvest and had asked Queen's for a student and the Land Army for a girl. The only volunteer that Queen's had was a young boy from Vienna, and the Land Army sent a girl who, although born in Ballymena, had an Italian name. So there assembled quite an international brigade on the farm.

Soon afterwards Mr. Moffat came to see me in the office one morning.

"You know this fellow Campbell in Portaferry?" he said.

"Yes."

"What sort is he?"

"Very decent."

"Pro-Nazi?"

"Good heavens no. Sure, he has his whole house full of refugees."

" That's just what is worrying Portaferry".

So I explained how there had come to be such a conglomeration of aliens on the farm, sent there by various agencies.

"Campbell was in Germany before the war?"

"So was I. Is that a crime?"

"No need to get on your high horse. Why has he grown a beard?"

"I really have no idea. I expect his wife has got tired hunting for razor blades." (They were scarce in the war.)

He laughed. "That's probably true. But it's not what Portaferry thinks."

"And what on earth is that?"

"They think, this young fellow Werner is his illegitimate son come to join him from Germany, and he has grown the beard to disguise the likeness."

"Well, all I can say is, I give Portaferry full marks for creative imagination."

I explained, of course, that Werner had entered this country as a twelve year old child, and that, to my certain knowledge, until the Committee had asked Philip to take the boy into his home, neither of them had ever clapped eyes on each other. He seemed satisfied.

But it was then that Werner did a dreadful thing: he became eighteen. From being a harmless refugee child, overnight he transformed himself into an enemy alien, and the first I knew of it was a letter from the police in Downpatrick wanting to know what he was doing in the Protected Area. Of course, it could have been argued that he was doing work of national importance, i.e. farming, but that was going to need a labour permit, and long before I was able to procure one, the police arrived and removed him. As he had nowhere to go, my father and I agreed to put him into our spare room. Eventually another home was found for Werner, but I felt it was a great pity that he had had to be moved just as he was beginning to enjoy the security of family life. I thought we should ask the police for their reasons, but other members of the committee with connections in Portaferry suggested that they would make some enquiries. At the next Committee meeting they said: "Maybe it's as well he's been moved as they say he's been seen walking along the shore with some very queer woman". This completely dumbfounded me, it was so unlike Werner.

Oskar was coming to supper that night and I asked him.

"Have you ever known Werner walk out with a girl?"

"Werner?" he said, "don't be daft, he wouldn't look at a girl."

"Portaferry says, he's been seen along the shore with a queer woman."

"They must be confusing him with someone else".

"Yes", I said, "Us. Remember the night we walked along the sea front and turned into Dumigan's? I am the queer woman. It must have been the Red Sails in the Sunset."

Aghast we considered what could be done, but as Werner was now settled in his new home, we decided to leave it. At least my red pants had not got him interned.

The Egyptian Princess was still with us and still perfectly normal when Werner occupied our spare room. One Saturday afternoon I was weeding in the flower bed outside the pantry window, when I overheard the pair of them chatting together. Werner, I don't think, had ever been to the pictures, he had never really had much opportunity and wanted to go, but was embarrassed that he had not the money for two. It was a delicate situation, but after much beating about the bush and dropping of hints they at last agreed to go Dutch and go together.

That evening at supper Werner seemed in very good form and I was glad to see it, because he had been very cast- down after being removed from the farm. After he had left the room, my father said: "Did I hear right? Is that young fellow who sat here at table with us now going to take the maid to the pictures?"

"He is", I said, "but for goodness sake don't say a word. If you knew how long it took them and how difficult it all was to reach such an agreement, you might inhibit Werner for life from trying to make a date with a girl."

My father only muttered about what the world was coming to, but said no more.

13

We announced our engagement at Christmas.

Every year there was a Christmas Party primarily for the refugee children and one or two others who could get themselves there. 0skar read the Christmas story from St. Luke in the German bible, then there was the *"Bescherung"*, the sharing out of little presents for everybody off the Christmas tree and then tea and wartime biscuits. After which we slipped away, telling the hostess she could announce our engagement when we had gone.

My father went to stay with his sisters and we went to the farm. But Christmas on the farm is very much the same as at any other time of the year. The same routine had to be followed, the animals have to be tended, but I always like to go to early service on Christmas Day and that presented problems. The only means of transport was a man's bicycle, and I had rather a tight skirt. However, with assistance I was mounted and wobbled off into the darkness, decently shrouded in a waterproof.

When I reached the church I got off by collapsing up against a bank and when I came out it was still dark - we had double summer time in wartime - so, waiting until the congregation had disappeared, I climbed the bank and got myself on again.

Dawn was breaking and far out at sea a silver streak lay across the water. Suddenly, as I sped along through the silent fields in the cold, exhilarating air, I felt so happy I started to sing at the top of my voice all the carols I new. There were lights in one or two cottages, but no one joined in.

When I got back to the farm, the others were busy milking, the storm lantern on the floor throwing gigantic shadows on the walls. The routine on the farm comes first and just when our goose, which had been filling the whole house with its delicious smell, had reached the table, the vet arrived in the yard to see a sick cow, and our dinner had to go back in the oven until he had finished.

We got married at Easter. As none of Oskar's family could be there, it was a very quiet affair in the little side chapel of St. Anne's Cathedral on our way to the Dublin train.

We spent our honeymoon in Hunter's Hotel in Wicklow. It is a quiet little place with a lovely garden sloping down to the river and apparently a favourite spot for honeymooners. Over the Easter week-end there came a flock of cyclists who had ridden down from Dublin, petrol being rationed, and as is frequent in such a group there is always one who wants to find out about everybody else There was one obvious honeymoon couple floating around hand-in-hand, and then her eye rested on us.

"I hear you're down from the North", she said, "what made you come here ?"

"We found it in the tourist brochure", I said, "an old coaching inn in a picturesque setting", and I thought it sounded nice. And then when we booked, they said we would have to move out across the river over Easter and I thought that some early morning exercise would be so good for my husband, so that clinched it."

"Not at all", she said, returning to the proprietress - with whom she had been discussing us, "those two have been married for years".

Recently we re-visited Hunter's Hotel. It is now run by a nephew and we told him we had spent our honeymoon there in 1943 He looked it up in the register and showed us our entry.

"And do you still have that little notice in your garden: 'Ladies and Gentlemen will not, and others must not, pick the flowers'?" I asked.

"You've a good memory", he said

"For things like that I certainly have".

He seemed very pleased and stood us a drink on the house.

My great-aunt Elizabeth and three of her children lived in Dublin. She had been outraged when her brother, my grandfather, the family fortunes having more or less dried up, moved into Belfast and entered business. She roundly declared that no son of hers would enter trade. Accordingly they all served in the British forces. She lost one in the Boer war and one in the Great war; cousin Arthur survived as a colonel in the R.A.M.C. Her attitude had left a certain coolness in family relationships, which was not improved by me at the age of about five flatly refusing to be bridesmaid at cousin Millicent's wedding. Earlier I had been bridesmaid when another cousin of my father's was married in Belfast. I was flanked on either hand by two little boys and we were instructed to kneel down when the rector said "Let us pray". But whereas I was dressed in a short frilly frock with bare knees and short socks, the boys' knees were encased in white satin pants and to them the wrath of Mum was much more real than the wrath of God. So when the moment came, no matter how I tugged and pulled, I could not bring those two young heretics to their knees. The whole church was convulsed by my efforts. My father afterwards referred to me as an early exponent of the church militant, which made me determined to have nothing further to do with grown- ups and their silly weddings. So my poor mother was left to write excuses about my bronchitis.

However, when Great-aunt Elizabeth's youngest son, having joined the R.I.C. came north and joined the R.U.C. after the Treaty, he and his wife became very friendly with us. They had no children of their own, but he adopted me in a way and made me many things for my doll's house, which I still have, all beautifully made, even a delicate little bird cage with a tiny bird inside. .

Nevertheless, something prompted me when writing to tell them of my engagement to describe Oskar as someone "whose father was Russian". I was not quite sure how they would take the news that in the middle of the war I was going to marry a German. However, passing through Dublin on our way home I invited ourselves to tea.

Great-aunt Elizabeth, who must have been nearly ninety and certainly was nearly bald, advanced down the room extending a claw-like hand to Oskar and saying "How do you do? I'm your mother-in-law". Whereupon her daughter rushed in to separate them, saying "No, no, mother dear, not mother-in-law", and to smile reassuringly at Oskar.

Cousin Arthur then asked in Russian, if Oskar spoke Russian. Oskar knows just enough Russian to be able to say that he does not, and the colonel continued "I was last in St. Petersburg on a military mission. St. Petersburg, not Petrograd, let alone Leningrad.

Meanwhile I was settled on the sofa with the old lady, who had grasped that I had not married a local.

"And have you known your husband long, dear?"

"Yes, several years".

"Oh, that's nice for you. And where are you going to live now?"

I explained about the shortage of houses and housekeepers and so we would live with my father.

"Oh, that's nice for you. And does your husband speak English? - That's nice for you".

And then we began again over the same three questions, each answer being greeted with, "Oh, that's nice for you".

I became aware that Arthur and Millicent (whose bridesmaid I had refused to be all those years ago) had run into difficulties with Oskar. They had discovered he had never been in Russia.

"Then, where were you born?" asked Millicent.

"In Germany".

"But you are not", she said in a sudden silence, "you are not *German*?"

I would liked to have chipped in "Actually he is Prussian", which was true, but I felt the last remnants of the British Raj in Dublin had had about as much as it could take for one day.

I must add that years later, when our daughters were at Trinity, Millicent who was then the sole survivor of the Dublin relatives became great friends with Susan, and when she died left her a legacy which allowed her to do a post-graduate course.

14

We returned to the farm that summer as husband and wife. In view of Oskar's previous experience, Philip had entrusted him with the running of the farm whilst he and Mabel went off for a fortnight's holiday with their little daughter Maeve. That Maeve was going too, was a relief to me. The Campbells had modern notions about rearing children; they very rarely said No, and considered that children should learn by experience. For instance, if Maeve went up the garden and ate green apples, she ought to have such tummy-ache that she would never do it again. That was the theory. In practice the child developed the digestion of an ostrich and nobody else got any ripe fruit. So I was quite happy I would not have to deal with Maeve.

Another relief, more to Oskar than to me, was that Philip had installed a milking machine and converted the old byre into a milking parlour. He only had twelve cows, yet milking that number by hand meant an early start in order to have the milk down at the end of the lane before the milk lorry came past. My job was to wash out and then with kettles of boiling water scald the big churns, which I did most conscientiously, and was therefore outraged when a ten-gallon churn was returned to us. In its journey down the lane in an open hand-drawn trekcart a tiny speck of mud had lit on its outside. How that could possibly contaminate the milk inside I could not imagine and can only think that some inspector somewhere wanted to prove how well he was doing his job. So we had milk puddings and custards, and all the cats had never had it so good.

The day before he left Philip had bought a new cow, and the Land Army went to introduce her to the milking machine.

"If this is the first time", said Oskar, "don't you think you ought to rope her hind legs? She might kick".

"I think she'll be all right", said the Land Army and bent down. Quick as a flash the cow kicked. The Land Army reeled back and sank unconscious to the floor. So we picked her up and carted her into the house where she revived on the sofa.

Presently there came a knock at the kitchen door. It was Alec to know if I would come and help. The cow had previously been owned and milked by a woman. Quickly I said Oskar was a much better milker than I was . But Alec said if she just heard a woman's voice beside her she might relax and let her milk down. So, diffidently I followed him out.

I remembered during the Nursery School's evacuation one of my family had had bad ears and I had tried to soothe her to sleep by gently massaging her forehead and endlessly singing or humming "Over the sea to Skye". I decided on the same technique with the cow.

So, whilst I fondled her ears and caressed the tufty little curls on the top of her head, keeping up a sleepy crooning, Oskar bravely applied himself to the business end. Gradually the fear faded out of her lovely eyes,.and, giving an enormous sigh, she shifted her weight so that her flank rested in a fold on Oskar's head, and presently we heard the cheerful chirp, chirp. chirp of milk filling the pail.

I had not brought my paints with me, but dipping a finger into a pot of white paint, I drew a rather Mae Westian cow with beautiful eyelashes on the byre door and labelled it "Milk Bar".

Next morning old Robert James, as he came up to work, stopped dead in his tracks in the middle of the yard and said: "Holy Jayses, who done thon? And the boss comin' home the morra!"

On the "morra" it was quite remarkable the number of people who had found themselves some little job to do, just sweeping up a few straws here or chivvying a few weeds there, but all within sight of the byre door. When Philip came out, fortunately he was pleased, so much so that when next the door had to be painted he would not allow my masterpiece to be painted over. He sold the farm a year or so later and the new owner apparently preserved my handiwork too.

On his new farm Philip went in for Jersey cattle and this time I painted several cows in pullovers simpering around, labelled "Latest Style Jerseys".

Mabel found one of the Transport Board's lorry drivers looking at it.

"Funny thing", he said, "I was making a delivery down the Ards the other day, and there's a farm there has the very same kind of thing".

Recognition at last!

But I am running too far ahead.

15

When we were engaged, I had wondered if Oskar would care for sailing and what I was going to do with the boat if he did not. Music was his thing. However, he said he had done some sailing and canoeing on the lakes around Potsdam. He had also played in the Berlin University orchestra when Schnabel had performed the Brahms Piano Concerto no.2. I mentioned that I had Schnabel with the BBC orchestra under Boult on records and lured him into helping me paint the boat with the promise of supper with Brahms to follow.

As it turned out, Oskar became an enthusiastic sailor. Petrol rationing had become so restricted that I had laid up the car and so we went down to Whiterock by bicycle. Once we rode down in the morning, sailed all afternoon and rode home in the evening. But we only did that once. After that we managed to get the loan of a caravan and stay over night and eventually we bought a second- hand caravan and found a plot near Whiterock. I remember the smell of honeysuckle as we sped down the Ballymartin Road towards Ardmillan with Strangford and its many islands spread out before us. Motorists enclosed in their cars must miss so much.

We spent many idyllic week-ends. Sometimes we would start out after breakfast, sail all day, landing on and exploring various islands, and return in the evening for the second meal of the day. Bird island was not then a protected bird sanctuary, and we were able to land and watch the young chicks chipping out of their shells, whilst the agitated parents swirled and swooped about us. Once or twice we sailed over to Kircubbin and asked at the butcher's for liver, which was unrationed, to be told that it was reserved for an evacuated school. We expressed our disappointment as we had just come all the way over from the other side. And the butcher, looking quickly right and left to see there was no one about, whispered "Would a couple of steaks do you?"

Later in the year we would return with mackerel for our supper, if we had been lucky enough to catch any.

For two summers we lived a kind of extended honeymoon, but by the third summer Anne had joined the party. She was a good baby and at eleven weeks adapted herself readily to life in the caravan, snugly tucked in her Moses basket. The war being over, although petrol was still rationed, we put the car back on the road, and so we were able to transport the baby and her bath and basket. But sailing was somewhat curtailed. One of us always had to baby-sit.

The next summer with Anne now fifteen months we decided on a different holiday. We would tour the Antrim coast as far as Ballycastle we hoped - that is if the car were strong enough to get the caravan up the hill after the Glendun viaduct. We spent our first night in Knocknacarry, but were disturbed in the night by cattle rubbing themselves against the caravan and kicking over one of Oskar's precious buckets of water. The next morning the car got us up on to the moors and we rolled pleasantly down towards Ballycastle. There were no caravan parks in those days and you just asked a farmer if you might park in his field, but this time

In the Mournes.

At a wedding.

we thought we would ask if we could park in a back yard, free from itchy cattle. We found such a farm which turned out to have been the dower house of the Casement family who lived nearby. The old father, who was crippled with rheumatism, hobbled up to us the next day and said:

"There's a couple of eggs for your tea". Eggs were still rationed.

We went to the beach, but Anne, after trying to eat the sand, had no further use for it. She was not very sure about the splashing sea waves either, so we took short drives in the car instead. We went up to Murlough Bay and, looking at the monument to Roger Casement, we noticed that one of the names inscribed at its base was the same as our host's. We wondered if it could be a relative.

"I wouldn't like to ask", I said, but Oskar was braver.

"Oh yes", said the girl, "that was Uncle Eddie. He was shot in 1916".

I thought what a strange place Ireland is. Either you regard Uncle Eddie as the black sheep of the family, in which case you would not allow his name to appear on a rebel monument within five miles of your home, or if you regard him as one of Ireland's holy martyrs, you do not go giving your Protestant visitors a couple of eggs for their tea. I doubt if you would allow them to camp in your backyard.

By the next summer Susan had joined the party. With the aid of a tent I attempted to cope. First I settled Susan, now in the Moses basket, in the tent and later put Anne into the camp bed beside her; (at ten o'clock we lifted them both and brought them in with us). But somehow, when getting Anne into the camp bed, we always managed to bump the basket and waken the baby who started crying, and then Anne started crying, because she could not get to sleep with that noise. Far out in the bay Oskar said he could hear me singing Ba Ba Black Sheep and both children bawling. And that really finished the caravan.

16

I thought it was time our little family had a dog, so I went to the Cats and Dogs place, which was then in a yard in May Street.

"Has he got a tail?" I asked, for the poor animal I was being shown had tucked it so tightly between his legs that I doubted that it was there at all. However, it was, and I took him home.

He was a brindle terrier about the size of a Kerry Blue with a white chest and a white tip to each of his four paws, and after he had had several good meals and walks he carried his tail in a magnificent curl, like a question mark.

In view of his mixed origins I tried to call him Grill, but found this did not trip easily off the tongue and settled instead for Curry.

"What breed is that dog of yours?" asked Mr.Payne, one of the older residents of Knockdene Park.

"A Heinz, I'm afraid", I said.

"M'm", he said approvingly, apparently accepting "Heinz" as a recognised breed, "a very fine looking dog. I've noticed him about in the Park."

And sometimes, when I saw Curry standing very erect and disdainfully permitting two of our neighbour's Corgis to sniff round him, I thought he looked the well-bred aristocrat and they, with their truncated bodies, the mongrels.

But he had a naughty habit of shadowing you when you went up to the shops at Knock Corner. When told to go home, he would appear to do so, but just as you reached the shops, there he was. This happened to Mrs. Neu, who lived with us then. The queue at the butcher's was right out across the pavement and all the dogs were attached by lead to their mistresses. This, to Curry, was a chance in a million and he soon had the whole queue inextricably tangled up in itself.

"He's not my dog", said Mrs. Neu, taking the belt off her coat, "but I know whose he is and I'll take him home."

"He's Mr.Atkinson's dog", said one outraged dame, "at least, I don't think it's Mr.Atkinson's, it's that Russian son-in-law's. You can see", she said self-righteously, "he's not one of *our* dogs.".

When this was related at home, Oskar said: "Poor Curry. Must have been the snow on his boots."

17

Things did not go well with me after Susan was born and I had to lie up for some time and have penicillin stuck into my behind until I felt like a pin cushion. On top of that we had domestic troubles as well, and whilst we tried to find a maid, a succession of elderly relatives came, briefly tried to cope and departed. One had a thing about cats and would only come, if we got rid of our beautiful Liquorice. So she was sent temporarily to the country where she ate rat poison and died. Curry disappeared. Whether he was run over or whether he walked out in disgust at another baby in the house we shall never know. And then the maternity nurse, who had been marvellous, was called to her next case earlier than expected; In fact I began to feel I was on ITMA. Hardly a day passed without someone popping their head round the door - "Boss, sumpin terrible's happened". Anne, who had been a model child always going to sleep as soon as she laid her little head on the pillow, became so upset with all the strange people putting her to bed that Oskar, who was then teaching in Banbridge and only came home at the week-ends, had to come home every night simply to get his eldest quietly to sleep. A grim time was had by all.

Nancy and Morris had once got a "treasure" from an agency in Eire, and in spite of our experience with the Egyptian Princess persuaded us to try again. "And if you can't get one, get two", said Morris, "the old man can pay". So we got two, aunt and niece supposedly cook and housemaid, and Morris volunteered to meet them off the train.

He came up to our bedroom.

"Well, what are they like?" I asked.

Morris was a kindly soul and when searching for words had a habit of rubbing his nose.

"They look", he hesitated, "and smell a little like ponies."

"That would be splendid, if it was ponies we wanted", I said.

Next morning they presented themselves at my bedside, and after the usual pleasantries I said "And which of you is the cook?" They looked at each other. Then Bridget, the niece, said: "Well, Annie knows the way to light the gas".

But that, as we soon discovered, was just about the extent of Annie's culinary knowledge. As I have already said, I could write a book on Maids I Have Known.

So we struggled on with me, as soon as I was up again, trying to keep ahead of each disaster, before it actually happened. Bridget, mopping in the fortunately empty nursery, knocked on the gas, but did not recognise the smell; Annie blew fuses in the washing machine. We had one of the older models of washing machines which had an open tub with a small electrically driven mangle above it. In vain did I counsel that before anything was fed into the mangle it must be seen to be free of entanglements, but invariably a sort of bird's nest would suddenly rise out of the tub and jam the mangle. Once Annie ran up the garden for help from the gardener who I doubt had ever seen a washing machine that was working properly, much less one that had gone berserk. Lifting his cap to scratch his head, he pronounced: "Now it doesn't take you to get excited with one o'them contraptions". Maybe not, but when one leg of Oskar's pajamas was winding round one of the rollers in one direction and the other round the other in the opposite direction, it is not easy to remain calm.

Fortunately the nurse had promised to come back to give us a long weekend to make up for having left us earlier than intended, and that was most welcome. I felt I needed a break.

When we came back, she said: "I don't want to alarm you, but I think those ladies are pregnant."

"Ah, go on, nurse", I said, "it's just your line of business. They are a bit thick round the middle, but they've probably been out working in the bogs or the fields heaving heavy loads".

"Next time the doctor's here, you should have them examined", she said.

In the end, that is what I did. Nurse was dead right.

So we discussed what was to be done.

"Do you know the father?" I asked.

Bridget nodded.

"Want to marry him?"

"Och indeed, I don't know. Me Da would kill me if he knew".

"You'll have to find somewhere to have the babies. Maybe the priest could advise you".

They came back from that interview somewhat chastened.

"That old boy has a right wicked tongue in his head", said Annie.

"Indeed 'twas terrible what he said to Annie."

Bridget, being younger, had apparently got off more lightly. Annie gave her head a defiant toss.

"I told him, if he couldn't help us, I'd give the child to the Salvation Army".

"And you should have heard him", said Bridget, holding her hand over her mouth in horror.

Next day they tried the Mater Hospital,.but were told there was no room for them and they should go to a hostel in Dublin. I told Bridget to ring the Mater and ask if they were certain the Dublin hostel would have room. Probably she had never used a 'phone before, anyway she came back in near hysterics, saying she had got the fire brigade, something I thought we could well do without.

When I had finished with the baby, I went to the 'phone.

"You mean to say, you have two of them in this condition?" said a chilly voice. "Well, really".

" I just want to make sure there'll be room for them in Dublin".

"I don't see what it's got to do with you".

I assumed, maybe wrongly, the chilly voice belonged to a nun. It is not often that the opportunity arises to tell a nun what you think her Christian duty should be, but instead I said: "They haven't been with me very long, so they can't have saved up very much money and if they spend it on going to Dublin and then find there's no room for them, what then?"

The chilly voice softened. "I shouldn't worry", she said, "even if they are full up, the Health Authorities aren't nearly so strict down there. They'll be able to fit them in".

So they went off to Dublin. Some months later Bridget - now more practiced with the 'phone - rang up. She said her baby had caught an infection and died and could she come back to me? But by that time I was struggling with yet another maid and felt I just could not take on Bridget again.

18

Oskar's sister Else had survived the war in relatively sheltered conditions in Apolda in Thuringia. She had been a head sister in a children's hospital, but when the Nazis took over had been dismissed, just as Oskar had been dismissed from the law courts. Her friend Greta, who was a doctor in the hospital and a very courageous woman, employed her privately as her children's Nanny, but by 1947 those two children were of school age and Apolda was in the Russian one. Else wanted to get out and we offered her the job of being Nanny to our two, and after weeks and weeks of writing and waiting and frustration she finally arrived.

Fortunately we got on very well together. At first her English was not very good and I suggested that she should talk German to me and I would talk English to her "so that at least we'll each know what we have said". It worked, although friends listening to our bilingual discussions of childish ailments wondered about the children's well-being. I realised that as far as children were concerned Else was the expert, but I did not want to hand them over entirely and so we took it in turns, week about, to do the cooking or the children and gave up the idea of looking for any more maids. From time to time we had part-time dailies of varying usefulness.

We had Sunday dinner in the middle of the day and when it was my turn to cook it, I went to St. Columba's in the evening.

When I went into the church one evening, I noticed what I thought to be a nun sitting at the back, and I thought I have seen people whom I know to be Methodists or Quakers in St. Columba's, but this is the first time I have seen a nun.

As I came out after the service, Mrs.Whitaker, the rector's wife, pounced on me.

"Ah, Mrs.Rudnitzky, you speak German, don't you? This is Schwester Marga from the Lutheran mission."

Schwester Marga's English at that time was not extensive and the sudden opportunity to speak German at somebody was like the release of Niagara. There we stood glued together in the middle of King's Road whilst the congregation dwindled away on either hand. I began to wonder how I could decently bring this encounter to an end. As we had had our main meal, I knew there would not be much for supper, probably only boiled eggs and salad, but I said she would be welcome. *"Gekochte Eier mit Salad!"* You would have thought I had offered smoked salmon with caviar. So we set off for Knockdene Park.

Oskar had been gardening and was now enjoying a snooze in the big armchair, hoping that sooner or later some of the females of his household would put a meal on the table.

"Wake up, my boy", I said, "Your number's up. There's someone here from the Lutheran mission. Wants to know why you haven't been." - A rude awakening.

Schwester Marga soon became a friend of the family and a frequent visitor. Else's English was making good progress, so she was able to help. They enjoyed chatting together, with me sometimes helping to disentangle them.

Her mission had been sponsored by the Presbyterian church, and one day I asked why it was that she came to St. Columba's.

“Because I like your service so much better. It is more like the Lutheran except for one thing. Why do your Protestant churches not have crosses on the table?”

“Well”, I said, knowing that it seemed a lame excuse and not one with which I agreed, “some people think we shouldn’t be too like the Roman Catholics.”

“But why not? You’re both Christians, aren’t you?”

To which I think there is no valid answer.

19

Now that we had someone reliable to look after the children, I began racing again. The club at Whiterock was expanding, yet the Snipe Class never regained its pre-war popularity, although we raced very keenly twice a week. I always fancied I was a better crew than skipper, having in the Snipe Championship of 1936 crewed for the then champion of England. I looked forward to having Oskar sail the boat, but although he now sailed very well, when it came to racing in moments of crisis he seemed to go blank about port and starboard and rights of way, and so it was really a relief to both of us when he said he thought I ought to carry on.

In those days at regattas the mark boats were often inhabited and if anyone infringed the rules whilst rounding the mark, they would have the rules explained to them in a way they were unlikely to forget. The starting and finishing lines were arranged for the benefit of the spectators on shore, and this usually meant a reaching start. You took the time as you crossed the line in the wrong direction, sailed for two and a half minutes and came back so that you ought to arrive on the line at gunfire, but the wind is never constant, it either freshens and you arrive too soon, or it drops light and you are late.

At Killyleagh regatta we arrived too soon. The whole fleet was packed in behind us with not an inch to dodge back into. I was commenting explosively on the situation, when the mark boat interrupted us:

“Come you on, Miss, you’re doin’ rightly”, it said.

“But we’re going to be too soon”, I said.

“Now, ye’ll be all right”, it said in the sort of tone you don’t argue with, if you have any sense.

I saw then that at the elbow of the voice stood the man with the gun.

So I came on - there was nothing else I could do anyway - and at the very moment, when our bow broke that invisible line from the mark boat to the flag on the harbour wall, there came a deafening explosion. By our stop watch it was a good two seconds too early and in fairness to our competitors I hope the watch was wrong, but sometimes I wonder. Probably the mark boat was reluctant to waste another cartridge on a recall. Anyhow, I have never before or since made a more perfect start.

We continued to enjoy racing for several more years, but the Snipe Class was dwindling, and in the end we sold Jenny Wren. She was bought by his guardian for the young Lord Erne and removed to Fermanagh, and I must say that as I saw her disappear I had a lump in my throat. For sixteen years I had had some great races with that boat.

However, with my cousin we chartered a Swallow at Cultra for part of the season from an owner who had to go to America on business. I understand that Cultra has greatly changed since then, but at the time I thought it was a very odd club. Before we were accepted as members, although we were allowed to race, we were not allowed to use the clubhouse. so we drove back to Knock in our wet clothes. I muttered darkly about doing a Lady Godiva act on their front lawn, but to Oskar's relief we were accepted as members before I put it into practice. Ladies went in by a separate door and only joined their menfolk in the dining room and very recently in the bar, but the course was pinned up to the main hall, where ladies were not allowed. I hovered outside the hall door until I saw someone I knew going in and was then handed out some unintelligible scribbles on the back of a cigarette carton with the result that twice we started in the wrong direction. They had lady members, mostly crews, but there were some who owned and raced their own boats, and you would have thought that they would have demanded equal status with the men in being able to study the course beforehand. Perhaps, like the Dublin ladies, they "always wanted to, but never dared".

Swallows are bigger and faster than Snipes, lively boats to sail, but for Oskar they had one great drawback: they had spinnakers. Once, when we had done rather well and got a gun, we swept over the finishing line in a stiff east wind with the spinnaker drawing for all it was worth, but then it jammed and refused to come down. We roared through the anchorage with Oskar tugging and jerking at it. I saw the mark at Holywood East looming up and thought the only thing that will stop us now will be the Queen's Bridge. But at last there came a crash of canvas on the deck. In moments of crisis we were always very polite, in fact, you could gauge the tension by the politeness.

I said: "Well now, dear, do you think I could come on the wind again and get back to the mooring, or is all that bird's nest going to go overboard?"

A voice from before the mast said: "Wish to hell, it would".

20

In the spring of 1950 the children, three of them by now, Barbara having joined the party, struck a patch of bad health and I decided a change of air might be a good idea. We could not afford to rent a house in July or August, and anyhow I did not want to wait till then, so we were lucky to find a reasonably rented house in May in Ballycastle in an almost ideal position, right on the sea front beside the golf course. There were no roads to cross to get to the beach. Oskar was then teaching in Annadale and came to visit us at the week-ends, sometimes bringing some of his colleagues with him. It was a large house with room for everybody.

The day after we settled in there came a flurry of snow - such is the outrageous behaviour of our weather - and Susan, then three, standing entranced at the window said: "Look at the lovely snow drops falling." After that the sun came out and thankfully the weather behaved more as it should in May.

From time to time a party of girls from the convent school came down on horses and enjoyed a canter along the strand, and I suddenly had a yearning to do likewise. Most of the horses looked pretty poor old things, long past their sell-by date, all except one. I enquired its name and where the stables were.

The next day I went to the stables and asked for that horse.

"Are you sure now that's the horse you want?" said the man, "it's not everybody can manage him."

"That's the one I want", I said.

He looked me up and down.

"Have you a stick with you?" he asked.

Having been brought up to believe "if you can't ride a horse with your hands and your heels, you're no bloody good" I said "No".

"You'd be the better for having a stick with you", he said and cut me one out of the hedge.

It was a lovely morning as I rode happily along the high ground above Ballycastle. That view as you drop down the steep hill at Quay Road is one of the finest on the Antrim coast. The sweep of the strand with the breakers running in, the green of the golf course and, in the background, the towering majesty of Fair Head.

I suddenly thought I might buy some fish for our dinner, if I went down to the harbour. I was doubtful if this horse, for whom a stick seemed necessary, would stand to let me on again if I dismounted, but fortunately the lady behind the slab of fish in the little shop was most obliging and came out to me. So with the fish in the paper bag we set off.

It was then that I discovered what was wrong with this horse. At some earlier stage some rough hand had ruined the left side of his mouth and try as I might nothing would make him turn left. Besides which he knew that home lay straight ahead up the Main Street.

We clattered and sidled all over the road - in those petrol-rationed days there was little traffic - and at one point he reared up in protest. I struck him sharply between the ears with the stick which at once broke. The fish was beginning to come out of its paper.

The old Marine Hotel, since burned down by the I.R.A., had surrendered its iron fence to the War Effort and all that was left was a kerb and a few iron stumps over which we stumbled. The horse showed a strong inclination to sit down on the window sill. Inside the manageress and her staff were at their morning coffee and they rushed out in some alarm.

"Could you just keep this fish for me while I deal with this horse?" I said, throwing them the disintegrating package.

Just then a man appeared from nowhere. Leading the horse firmly by the head until he got us facing the right way, he then hit the horse an enormous wallop on its behind. We shot off at full gallop up the middle of the road past the tennis courts, leaving me breathless but most grateful.

The children were intrigued with the horse, although they kept their distance, whilst I explained to Else the whereabouts of our intended dinner. The horse responded without alacrity to a canter along the strand, but the minute I turned to go back I had to hold him hard.

21

It was about this time that Philip sold his farm at Portaferry to my surprise. I had grown fond of Ballycam and thought that Philip had put a lot of work into improving the land - he once described farming as the most gentlemanly way of losing money. But they wanted to send their children to school in Friends' School in Lisburn and they bought a farm at Killultagh near Glenavy. It was a pleasant old house, two hundred or more years old, solidly built with deep set windows with interior shutters. It had two magnificent beech trees on its front lawn, which sheltered it from the winds which swept across Lough Neagh and up the gently sloping fields, but also sheltered it from the sun and screened what should have been a lovely view over part of Antrim and Down to the distant Mournes or over Lough Neagh to the Sperrins. You had to go outside into the fields to appreciate its lovely position.

Once again the Campbells asked us to look after the place whilst they took their children to the sea for a fortnight.

Philip now employed just one old man, Fergie, who lived at the bottom of the lane in a semi-detached cottage. In the other half lived Harriet, who came up to clean on Wednesdays, but long ago these two had quarrelled; what it had been about no-one could remember and, as sometimes sadly happens in Ulster, they vowed never to speak to each other again. It seemed very sad to me that these two, both no longer young, should live side by side in silent bitterness.

Mabel had left me copious instructions which directed when giving them their dinner on Wednesdays to put out everything in duplicate, two teapots, milk, sugar, butter, jam and cruets because they would never ask the other to pass anything. She also added: "Don't give Fergie raspberry jam. He says the pips get between his teeth", which seemed to me an unnecessary advice. So far as I could see, he only had three teeth in his head, one above and two widely dispersed below. However, I put out some of Mabel's rhubarb am.

But one day when the service hatch between the kitchen and the dining room had been left open, we did hear Fergie speak. The collie bitch had just whelped and she and her pups were in a box beside the range, and Fergie said: "Harriet" (he pronounced the first syllable as in 'hard'), "Harriet, d'ye see what one o'them pups is doin' on yer clean floor?" In the silence that followed we could hear the squeak and tapping of Harriet's knife and fork and imagine her tightly compressed lips. Then Fergie said: "Faith, I think if I was doin' the like o'yon, ye'd find somethin' to say to me".

On our first morning, after I had probed the mysteries of the kitchen range, I emerged with the ashes and was wondering where they should be put, when there came something like a sub-terranean rumble from the byre, which resolved itself into Fergie's voice. "Ye'll find a wee pad fornenst the door." My heart warmed to Fergie at once. Lovely Ulster word, that 'fornenst', so much more concise than 'opposite to' or 'over against'. Fornenst says it all in one. It has a Nordic flavour. I would like to think we got it from the Vikings, but I have not found it in any modern Scandinavian dictionary. So perhaps it is our very own.

That summer was one of those summers which we sometimes have, when there is a water shortage. In Killultagh House the machine which charged the electricity also pumped the water, and after Oskar had switched it on one morning, he disappeared with Fergie. Shortly afterwards I was horrified to see the overflow pipe spluttering water over the roof. It was not doing the old roof any good, and in a time of shortage such waste was wicked. I had no idea how to stop the machine, so I started shouting for Oskar and running towards the distant sound of a tractor.

The funny thing about tractors' noise is that people on it have to shout into each others' ears, but yet their voices can carry across fields. Just when I thought I would never make them hear me, I heard Fergie's voice "Thonder's the missus. Shoutin'." I turned sideways and mimed the blowing up of a bicycle tyre.

"It'll be the pump", came Fergie's voice.

I stood up and made expansive circling movements with my arms.

"I doubt she's overflowing".

I made vigorous 'come hither' signs and the tractor turned towards me.

"Aye, when we heard the shouting", said our neighbouring farmers, "we were nearly coming up. We thought the house was on fire."

The next summer we were again at Killultagh. Harriet had become interested in us and questioned Else about our name and how we had arrived here. Else explained , but found that Harriet did not know very much about refugees. However, she added that I had been born in Belfast.

"D'ye tell me that, now?" said Harriet, "I would hardly credit that, for don't ye know, she's like used on a farm". "Used on a farm", now this was praise indeed. For days afterwards I walked about several inches taller. But my new-found status was sorely tried on the following Wednesday.

In Ballycam the kitchen stretched across the breadth of the house; one window looked out on the lane, the other on the yard, so that you had ample warning of the approach of visitors. In Killultagh one window looked into the shrubbery and the pantry jutted out to screen the other from the yard, so the only indication that someone had arrived was the fury of the dogs and the pandemonium amongst the hens.

Harriet went out to see and returned to say: "Yon's the transport men. They want to know where you want the farn crate put."

"I'd better go and see them", I said, disguising the fact that I had no idea what kind of a thing a "farn crate" might be.

"What is it you have brought?" I asked. This time it sounded more like a farrow in a crate. But that did not seem to make sense because, so far as I could see, there was nothing whatever in the crate.

"I'd better find one of the men", I said, again cloaking my ignorance. Anyhow that sounded very grand as if we had a whole retinue of farm labourers instead of just Fergie and Oskar.

Down the back lane I found Fergie.

"The transport men have brought something and want to know where it is to go"- I said.

"What is it?" said Fergie. (I had hoped he would not ask that.)

"It sounds like a farrow in a crate", I said diffidently, knowing that that could not be right.

"Och aye, that'll be for the ould sow", said Fergie. And at last the penny dropped. But for anyone who is as ignorant as I was on that summer's day I should explain that when a pig gives birth, it is called farrowing, her progeny are called her farrow - I should have remembered that James Joyce allowed Daedalus to say that Ireland was a sow who ate her own farrow - and because she is likely in the pangs of child birth to throw her considerable weight violently about and sometimes crush some of the new-born piglets against the sty walls, a farrowing crate has been devised with safety hatches round its base, allowing the piglets to escape from mamma's convulsions.

That was the summer when, earlier in the year, I had been smitten by a slipped disc. Until that happened I had thought of slipped discs as a fancy name for lumbago, but found unfortunately that this one did not respond to any of the recommended treatments and took nearly six months before it wore off. So by evening, when the children had been got to bed, I was quite content to sit knitting by the kitchen range, whilst Oskar went off alone to shoot hares, of which there were many. We always shot for the pot, not for sport, and my jugged hare went down well.

One evening shortly after the delivery of the farrowing crate, as I was sitting by the fire, I became aware that there were extraordinary noises coming from the pig sty and I went out to investigate. The first door I opened revealed a much startled pig, her floppy ears which usually fell over her eyes were standing out stiffly and her tiny eyes looked as if they would pop out of her head, but the squeals were coming from the next door sty, and when I opened that door, the first thing I saw was a little pink piglet. I shut the door quickly and, hobbling off as fast as my disc would let me, I shouted for Oskar. I no longer cared if the neighbours thought the house was on fire again. Fortunately Oskar was not too far away and came at once.

For the next hour or so Oskar, in the manner of a good scrum-half, slung each new arrival out to me and I deposited it safely in the far corner of the sty, and at the end of that time we had assembled twelve little pink piglets and only lost one poor misshapen little thing which would have died anyway. We had had a lucky let-off, but we did not feel very pleased with ourselves as shamefacedly we slunk off to bed past the unused crate still standing in the yard. We had forgotten to read the dates in the diary Philip had left for us.

22

Whilst we still had Else to look after the children, we thought that we could have a holiday on our own, just the two of us. There were still currency restrictions, limiting the account of money you could take out of the country, so we planned to spend the greater part of the time living as cheaply as possible in Hintertux, in a small village in the Tyrol, and then have three nights in Salzburg.

Hintertux was a charming little place with only one small hotel, so that by the end of our three week stay we had formed a nodding acquaintance with nearly everyone - in fact, entering the dining-room became like the finale of the pantomime when you had to remember to bow to right and left and there was a great deal of heel-clicking amongst the men. We got chatting to an elderly gentleman with courtly manners, a gynaecologist from Stuttgart, who seemed to know a lot about the life in the forest. He introduced us to *Pfefferlinge*, the woodland mushrooms, which if you gathered them the hotel would cook for you and which were delicious. He explained in his faulty English that in his younger days he went hunting (as they call shooting) in the mountains and that it was a noble sport shooting chemists! He meant chamois (in German *"Gemse"*). After we had sorted that out Oskar delicately suggested that as his wife understood German quite well it might be easier if we used that language

He had been a member of the Nazi party. That did not surprise us very much - many people had to become at least nominal members in order to keep their jobs, but gradually it became clear that he thought the only thing wrong with Nazism was that it had failed. He greatly admired the Duke of Windsor whom he considered to be a friend of Germany. "If he had been king, there need never have been a war".

"But you don't condone the concentration camps and the gas chambers," we said.

"That is all British propaganda".

"And the mass graves that have been found?"

"Air raid victims ".

I said, with Oskar helping me along, "Look, I've been secretary of a refugee committee which had two young girls in its care After the war someone who had been with their parents in the concentration camp wrote to tell them how brave their parents had been up till the mother's health had broken down and the father did not care anymore and both had been exterminated. Why should anyone bother to do all that if it wasn't true?"

He had no answer to that and probably wrote me off as brainwashed. Later he was joined by a younger man.

We were also going for walks with a couple from Paris; he was Irish and had served in the Irish Guards in the first World War, she was French and their son in the last year of the second war had just been commissioned in the Irish Guards. He was present at Rommel's last counterattack in the Ardennes. Things were fairly hot when three German prisoners were brought in and the commanding officer said to their son, "we cannot spare anyone to take these men to the rear, so if things get worse, you have your revolver, you know what to do.". As soon as he had gone, the young chap said to an orderly, "Take these men to the rear".

"But, sir, isn't the major only after saying...."

"I'll take full responsibility". I could have cheered. So often Nazi atrocities had been explained, because they were obeying orders from above.

The next day their son was ordered before the Brigadier.

"It has been reported to me that on the field of battle you disobeyed your commanding officer."

"I'm sorry, sir, but I am a Catholic and I cannot carry out such an order. If you wish, you may have my commission." Which, had it been accepted, would nearly have broken his father's heart- but it wasn't. The Brigadier muttered something about a serious offence and nothing more was heard.

Sometimes we all sat together in the evenings. The Parisians spoke French and English, The Germans German and some English and we acted as the link between. We discussed many things, and once the younger German, who had served in the army in France, admitted that he had seen things being done which made him ashamed of the German army. Next morning the old boy drew us aside and said we should not believe everything he told us. He was not really a German his mother was Austrian! Heigh ho.

On our last night we asked the proprietress, who was German, to join us for a drink. "And which of all the nationalities do you find the most difficult?" we asked.

With a quick look round she whispered *"Die Wiener"* (the Viennese).

We had to start very early next morning to catch a bus down the valley to the train. Already the farmers were at work scything the hay on the high Alpine meadows and, to judge by the length of the swathe behind then, they must have begun at the first light of day. They pack the hay into big bags and send it whizzing off down the mountainside on wire cables.

The distance, as the crow flies, is not great from Hintertux to Salzburg, but the train wends its way round mountains and through (by tunnel) and does not arrive until the afternoon. So, as tickets are not cheap in Salzburg, we decided not to book for anything on our first night, in case we arrived feeling too tired and sleepy to appreciate the music. But when we arrived, we felt surprisingly fresh and found that the *"Merry Widow"* was being given by an opera company from Vienna, and there were still a few seats left. It was a sparkling performance, given with all the verve and charm of light-hearted Viennese gaiety, in which the cast seemed to enjoy themselves as much as the audience.

The next day we had a more serious concert, Mahler's Fahrender Geselle, conducted by Furtwangler, in which the soloist was a youngish man, whose name we did not know, but who, we agreed, had a very fine voice: Dietrich Fischer-Dieskau.

And on our third night we went to a stunning performance of Othello, an opera I had never seen before. The whole production, the music, the scenery, the costumes and the staging were superb. The technique of running a film behind the backdrop of the stage was new to me, so that in the first act, when Othello comes ashore after his victories, the breakers were bursting beyond the harbour and storm clouds were scudding across the sky.

Salzburg has a number of very attractive medieval cellars, where they appear to serve meals all night long, and we had arranged with some friends from Belfast to meet in one of them after Othello, to which we were all going.

As we sat down together, everyone around the table was raving about the performance we had just enjoyed. But I have a very peculiar musical digestion; music that I have heard tends to repeat itself on me after a two day interval, and as I sat there, I thought "If anyone round this table could hear what is going on in my head, I don't think they would ever speak to me again".

"Jetzt geh' lch zum Maxim,
Da tu' ich sehr intim,
Ich grüsse alle Damen,
Ruf sie beim Kosenamen,
Lulu, Shushu, Froufrou ..."

23

At the same time as our youngest, Barbara, started school, Else underwent a serious operation and afterwards went for a long visit to her sister in South Africa, leaving us to cope with our three daughters on our own. I well remember our first Christmas after she had gone. Susan, then about seven, had developed sinus trouble and was behaving very much as I had done at that age with frequent tummy upsets, when the thought of any excitement, such as a Christmas party or a visit to the pantomime, sent her temperature up, before we got near either.

We had got a cat again, but we did not know that cats love to do what they should not under the Christmas tree, so that while Oskar, armed with mop and bucket, chased the cat round the tree, I was dashing hither and thither with basins to Susan. Suddenly we heard the Fire Brigade.

Susan sat up in bed, suddenly revived.

"Oh mummy, listen. I do hope they come to us."

Once again I thought it was something we could well do without.

And when Barbara lost her first baby tooth, I placed it in a glass of water to be replaced by a sixpence by the fairies in the belief that the shock of the cold water on her fingers would waken her and she would not in a drowsy state play with or possibly swallow the sixpence.

While it was still dark, a little figure stood sniffling in our doorway.

"I've lost my sixpence".

"Never mind, Bar, we'll look for it when it's light".

"But I've swallowed it", she wailed.

Well, I shook out the bed clothes, got a torch and grovelled about under the bed, even under the carpet, but no sixpence was to be found.

After breakfast I rang the doctor.

"There is one way to find out", he said, take her up to the Children's Hospital and have an X-ray."

Susan was already in the hospital, undergoing treatment for her sinus, and she and all the rest of her ward were intrigued with Bar's accomplishment, as were the nurses. Her fame echoed before us as we went along the corridor, with nurses swooping on Barbara, exclaiming "And is this the wee girl that's swallowed the sixpence?"

Barbara resented her fame. "Mum" , she whispered, "don't tell any more people or they'll have it in the papers.

When eventually we saw the X-ray, there for all to see was the sixpence. The doctor complimented Bar on her digestion at having got it as far as she had in the time and assured me that it would turn up in the course of nature, and then added: "You can put it in next year's Christmas pudding".

It did turn up eventually, but we did not put it in the pudding.

About this time we went for a week-end to Cushendun. A group of children were digging in the sand and I watched Anne circling them, hoping to be invited to join in. Years earlier in the Kindergarten in Strathearn she had overheard a child saying: "Don't ask Anne Rudnitzky to your party. Her father's a German!" It made Anne, a shy child, uncertain of her reception from other children; she would like to know how she would be received before making an advance.

Anne

Susan

Barbara

Once upon a time

However, on the beach at Cushendun she eventually made up her mind and dropped down beside them.

In a few minutes she came back to me.

"Mum, are we Protestants?"

"Yes. Why?"

"They said they couldn't play with me, because we were Protestants and they were bad people".

I suppose I should have gone over and had a chat with the children, but you don't always do what you ought to do. Maybe, I too was a little doubtful about the reception I might get. Instead I just grumbled to myself "The Rudnltzkys always seem to be on the wrong side of some blessed fence."

As a half-term treat at Hallowe'en we invited as many children as could be packed into two cars and took them to Scrabo. I went in advance and laid a paper chase up through the woods at Klllynether and we turned the children out at the bottom and met them, when they arrived panting at the top. In those days two elderly sisters acted as caretakers. They lived at the bottom of the hill, but every day toiled up the long climb and cleaned the tower meticulous1y. They kept hens and goats at the top, but otherwise must have carried up all their other provisions, yet if telephoned beforehand they provided a real farmhouse tea with scones and barnbracks and pancakes, all produced on an old-fashioned range, which nearly roasted us too.

As we drove home, a sleepy voice in the back of the car said, "I know what the three Miss Rudnltzkys are going to do when they grow up. They're going to live in Scrabo and give tea to people".

All mothers know what it is like trying to keep a convalescent child amused when they are really well enough to be up. Everything you suggest is turned down: 'have read all those stories; can't draw a picture, the point's broken; there's a bit missing out of that jig-saw' and so on.

Such was the case with Anne, then about nine, when one evening I was struggling downstairs to get supper into the oven before Oskar came home. In a frenzy I dashed into the sitting room and my eye fell on The Oxford Book of Comic Verse, after which such a silence fell on the house that I began to wonder if anything had happened. That dressing gown on the back of the door, she might have been twiddling with the girdle, put it round her neck - silly sort of thing a bored child might do - and reached out and overbalanced. It was not long before I was up the stairs once more.

And there she was with nothing whatever the matter.
"Mum, listen to this:
'Lizzie Borden with an axe
Hit her father forty whacks,
When she saw what she had done,
She hit her mother forty-one.'"
That put me in my place.

24

As the eleven-plus loomed up ahead of Anne, the youngest of Morris's daughters outgrew her pony and he offered him to us. Whilst we were considering this possibility, Miss Maxwell of Richmond Lodge tipped the scales by saying "And if you parents are thinking of offering a reward, give it to your child now before the exam." So Dick joined the family.

He was a Thelwell type, plump with a nimble leg at each corner, but he was a splendid children's pony, very game and devoid of tricks. He had an intelligent head and sized up precisely what had to be done about the various obstacles the Pony Club set in his way and he safely piloted all our daughters through these events. I sometimes liked to think there might have been a drop of Arab about him, although it was known that his mother drew a vegetable cart round Holywood.

And so, a year or so later, Dick took Anne to her first hunt. It may be wondered at how much I must have changed from the child who snapped mousetraps to an adult who condoned hunting. I confess I myself had hunted, I confess I had enjoyed it, although what I enjoyed most were the drag hunts at the end of the season where no animal was involved. I admit that hunting is a cruel and inefficient way of reducing vermin, yet when you have learnt to ride you want to put what you have learnt to the test across country.

The meet was at Lisbarnet School, very near where we now live. Anne and Dick set out to hack from Dundonald, where we had grazing for Dick, and I followed with her sisters in the car. When we got there we found that Dick was beside himself with excitement; he was dancing about on his tiptoes, sweating badly and giving little hops just to show how he would like to buck if he weren't such a nice pony. Probably if he had been able to have a bit of a gallop, he would have settled down, but the hounds just waggled their tongues and their tails and failed to find anything to chase. The whole circus trampled over a number of fields on one side and then on the other, but the hares seemed to have left the district. And so, as Dick was giving Anne an uncomfortable ride, we decided to call it a day. I handed Anne the sandwiches I had brought and started her to walk Dick quietly towards Comber, and when the rest of us had eaten our sandwiches, I turned the car and followed.

We had not gone far when we came on a horse-box drawn up at the side of the road with a lady and gentleman and Anne, very white-faced, all looking at Dick, who was lying on the road.

The lady advanced and, putting her head in at the window, breathed alcohol over us and said: "You know, that little pony of yours is just dying of colic".

Whereupon Bar wailed "Oh Mummy" and turned her face from the scene.

The gentleman turned out to be Mr.Ferguson, the vet. in Newtownards. "If you just follow me back to the surgery, I'll give you a bottle that'll settle him." And at that Dick showed signs of reviving and struggling to his feet, was turned into a field.

"How do I give it to him?" I asked in the surgery. I was thinking of the story of the man who went to give his horse a pill by blowing it through a tube, but the horse coughed first.

"There were a couple of old farm hands there. If they're about when you get there, they could do it for you", he said. I sincerely hoped they would be about.

When we got back, I found the hedgerow was lined with spectators, all gazing at Dick, who, always a greedy little pony, was trying to wolf as much grass as he could before anyone stopped him.

An elderly countryman slid out of the hedge. "He'll be all right now", he said, "he's passed his water".

I had no idea that was the moment they were all waiting for, but thankful that the medicine did not seem to be necessary.

So we re-arranged ourselves. Susan was to lead Dick into Comber, whilst Anne had a brief rest in the back of the car, before being set down in Comber Square to wait for Dick. She would then sit on him and walk to Dundonald, whilst Susan got a bus home. Our day was further complicated by a pupil of Oskar's, Robin Morrow, coming to collect one of our kittens. Meantime I would dash off with Barbara who was due at a school friend's party in Ballylesson at three-thirty. "Although I don't really feel like a party, I'm too upset", she said, looking disconsolately out of the window.

Oskar was enjoying his Saturday afternoon's snooze when we rushed in and related these misadventures. When I had delivered Barbara to her party, I persuaded him that we could leave Robin Morrow and the kitten to Susan, when she came off the bus, and that he should come with me to meet Anne in case she needed help with Dick. She was almost at Dundonald when we met her and all was well, but as I turned the car I heard that ominous little ticking of the petrol pump and hoped we would make it to the garage. We did not. Within sight of the garage, just at the fork of the Comber and Newtownards roads, we died. Oskar fetched a can of petrol, and just too late I said: "Keep some to prime the pump", after which there was nothing for it but to push. By then it was dusk and the Saturday evening traffic was streaming out of Belfast. Indignant motorists tooted and flashed their lights, but putting our heads down we pushed on doggedly across the Comber road to the garage, and fortunately no pile-up occurred.

Once home, Anne skipped off for a bath and I turned to thoughts of supper.

"I think you could do with a glass of sherry", said Oskar. It seemed a long time since I had gobbled those sandwiches, a great deal had happened since and the effect of that one glass was quite remarkable. Under the impression that I was grilling sausages I found myself performing a kind of gavotte, to and fro with the stove, at which point the electricity failed, leaving me in the dark, ankle-deep in black kittens.

Altogether it had been quite a day.

25

Our family were beginning to want seaside holidays, although they had always enJoyed themselves on the farm at Killultagh, and so for three years we went to Donegal. We were on a fairly tight budget which prohibited staying in hotels; twice Oskar, who was then teaching in Annadale, went abroad with a party of his pupils, whilst I and the children stayed at various houses in the Marble Hill, Port-na-blagh area. All that children need is a beach, preferably with rocks and pools as well as sand, and other children. I had always avoided resorts which offered ice-cream, candy floss and amusement arcades, which simply transformed children into yammering little gold diggers.

We were staying in Marble Hill when electricity came to Donegal, and the children were quite disappointed to see the candles and oil lamps which had so fascinated them being put away. It had become a tradition with us that on the last night of the holiday we should have a camp fire sing-song, and with the other children of our 'house' we cadged a few potatoes to roast from our landlady and settled ourselves in the heather. As darkness fell, we could see people in the cottages round about standing at their lighted doors listening to us, and then suddenly after what we had agreed was to be the last song one of the boys, who was English, struck up "The Queen". We all sang it, after which I said: "Come along, children, bedtime", and bundled everybody off home, not being very sure what the local reaction might be.

Next morning, as we went down for our last swim, the cottagers were at their doors. "We enjoyed your singing last night - especially the last item", and beamed at us.

26

From what I have saId about sailing at Cultra it is clear that it was not our favourite spot. There are no interesting islands to take the family to explore and when Philip Bell invited us for a day on Strangford with his family I knew what we were missing. I enquired if he knew of a cheap family boat and he said: "Well, Ocean Spark is lying in our backyard". Long ago he had first learned to sail in her and had always had a soft spot in his heart for her, but she had spent most of the First World War lying on her side, acting as a potato clamp, from which she had contracted a chronic leak.

I well remembered her at the time of the Snipe Class Championship in 1936, when the new clubhouse at Whiterock was being opened and the Committee were moved to tidy the place up. Ocean Spark was lying half submerged, neglected by her then owner, a sight which went to Philip's heart. So a gang of strong young men was raised, Ocean Spark was bailed out, put on a carriage and winched up the slipway, no mean achievement with a waterlogged boat. The houses opposite the clubhouse had not yet been built and it was intended to push her across the road into the field, but after she was halfway through the gate, she refused to budge any further. The crowd of helpers grew. They oiled the wheels of the carriage and scraped away stones that might be stopping her and finally said: "Now all together", and a pack of rugger-playing types put their heads down and pushed. To the twang of recoiling telephone wires Ocean Spark shot into the field. When the telephone people came round to repair the damage, very few of us were about.

And now, when I saw her again some twenty years later, I thought she would suit our purpose very well. She was the sole survivor of the Dublin Bay Colleen Class, built about 1880, with a large mainsail, as was fashionable then, and a small jib, partially decked and, although clinker built, she had graceful lines, but her great advantage was that, when her heavy old iron centreplate was raised, she only drew eighteen inches. The perfect picnic boat.

"She still leaks a bit", said Philip as we drove away with her. She did.

At first we tried every remedy known for leaks; some previous owner had gummed all round the base of her centreplate casing with a sticky mixture of tar, but still she leaked. Once, just after we had launched her and were getting the carriage back up the slipway, a friend who worked in Harland and Wolf's said "Look at your boat". I turned just in time to see her mast heel over and disappear. "I've waited all my life to see that happen in the Yard", he said. After that we tried a different scheme. We moored her above a nice muddy patch with no stones or rocks to damage her bottom and allowed her to fill and sink, visible at low tide but completely submerged at all other times for about a fortnight. Then the whole family, armed with buckets, was mobilised to paddle out to her at about twenty minutes before dead low tide and begin sloshing water out of her in all directions in the hope that she would float on the incoming tide, her seams having closed. She did.

By now we had rented a small cottage near Sketterick and the children invited their schoolfriends to stay. One mother was heard to remark that she really hesitated to let her daughter join us, "they have such an unseaworthy boat". Nevertheless, once Ocean Spark had "taken up"as they say, she never leaked more than could be dealt with by the pump. We landed on islands, just as Oskar and I had done years before, and the children were delighted to see the chicks chipping out of their eggs as the seagull parents screamed around us. Once` we had eleven human beings, a dog and a large picnic basket in that boat.

27

Anne was growing apace and soon her long legs hung down below Dick's fat little tummy. So we acquired a bigger pony whom, as she had come from Co. Clare, we called Clarissa. We had grazing for them on a farm on the Old Dundonald Road, near where the Ice Bowl is now, and for the summer holidays we got grazing at Whiterock. The migration was quite something. We never possessed anything like a horse box, but with the co-operation of a schoolfriend of Susan's, who liked riding, two children started out to ride to Whiterock and we followed in the car some time afterwards with everything else, including the dog and the cat with all her kittens in a box. When we overtook the riders along the Comber road, they were replaced by the two we had in the car. That was the method we employed to reach all the Pony Club rallies, so that no one got too tired having to ride all the way.

The cottage had electricity, but no running water, it had a range and a nice old Welsh dresser on which the crockery was displayed.

One Easter we came down to find the chimney blocked by a bird's nest, We hoked and poked to no avail and decided to get on the roof and poke downwards, but we had no ladder. Eventually we managed to throw a rope right over the house and whilst all the family held on on one side, Susan climbed up the rope on the other side, even although Bar kept on letting go to run round and see how she was getting on. The nest was an old one which the birds had abandoned, because it had already slipped down into the chimney and was impossible to hook up. So, various heavy objects, including a large horseshoe on a string were passed up to Susan to try to dunt the nest down. But these slipped off the string and remained stuck in the chimney. Some day, if that chimney ever comes to be rebuilt, it will be interesting to see what theories about the local folk-lore which caused the cottagers to keep horseshoes in their chimneys will be advanced.

In the end 0skar said if we made a big enough fire below we could burn the nest out. It worked, but was not his most popular idea. Long before the nest caught fire, the whole cottage filled with smoke and all that crockery had to come down off the dresser and be washed. And the water had first to be pumped and then heated on the range.

We used to take the ponies to be shod at a forge, now falling into ruin, at Derryboye. It was worked by a nice old man and his nephew in complete silence. We thought he communicated what he wanted his nephew to hand him by the taps he gave the anvil. He said he had had one day's holiday in his life, when he went to Newcastle.

At about this time the yacht club at Whiterock had a steward, who was an excellent man with the boats. He was an ex-navy man and like many such he had never learnt to swim, so that when he had to go out on rough days he fortified himself with Dutch courage. And sometimes on other days too, which so infuriated his wife that she would chase him out of the club, whereupon he simply got on his motorbike and went up to Johnnie's at the crossroads.

From time to time the Committee had him on the mat about these unseemly scenes, but because, although he might be quite unsteady on land, afloat he manoeuvred the club launch so skillfully, they never got round to sacking him.

There used to be a very dangerous S-bend - now much improved - in the middle of Killinchy village with the high stone wall of the Glebe lands on one side. One day returning from the forge at Derryboye I thought as we were nearly home I could leave the children and go on ahead to start getting dinner, when round the corner, already on if not over the white line, came the steward on his bike. I trod on everything and stopped dead. He gave a wobble and then, passing across my bow, somehow squeezed between me and the Glebe wall. I watched him in the mirror wending his wavering way down the hill until I saw he was safely clear of the children.

When next I saw him in the club I said: "Is that the way you usually get round that corner?"

"Oh, was it you, ma'am? I didn't see who the lady was. You won't tell on me, will you, ma'am?"

I said: "No, I won't tell on you. But I'll tell you this. There's a limit to the number of times you'll come round that corner like that and live".

"Indeed you're right, ma'am, indeed you're right. When I got down to Johnnie's, they said 'what ails ye? You're as white as a sheet.' And do you know, I was just shaking."

"And lucky you were. You might well have been stiff."

"Indeed you're right, ma'am", and so he continued. I shall return to this tale later to explain how votes are won in elections. It has nothing whatever to do with political ideologies.

28

Anne and Susan settled happily into life at Richmond Lodge, but Barbara, much to my disappointment, proved to be the odd one out. I blame my old school a little bit for reproaching her with "when your sisters were in this class, they would never have handed in work like this", which simply put her back up. Soon she almost ceased to hand anything in at all. I need not now record all the bother there was about homework and books left in school or left at home (at least well out of range of the person who ought to have been using them), but eventually Miss Maxwell and I held a serious consultation. We agreed, although neither of us favoured boarding schools, that in Barbara's case it might be better. This was a severe blow. Boarding schools cost money and we had not got a lot of that. However, we eventually settled for Drogheda Grammar School. It was an old Protestant school where the Duke of Wellington and Henry Grattan had been educated and which had been in decline when the Society of Friends thought it a pity that it should fold and decided to support it and admit girls. It never became a Quaker school, although the headmaster and his wife were both Quakers from England. It was not a large school and we liked its atmosphere.

As the new housing estates devoured the fields between us and Dundonald, grazing was getting increasingly difficult to find. At first we had been with Mr. Robb of Robb's Road, but he did not like the children riding on Sundays, he was an elder in the Presbyterian Church in Dundonald, and we were lucky to find a farm almost opposite where the Ice Bowl is now. I preferred to have the ponies on a farm where I knew someone would keep an eye on them, but when that farm decided to put more cattle on the land, we were really hard pressed to find anywhere to put the ponies. Eventually I settled for a piece of ground scheduled for building, but unfortunately the grazing was poor. The ponies hankered after the lush pastures of their previous lodging and kept breaking out and returning to it by trotting along the old disused railway line. I tried to supplement their feeding with pony nuts and hay. It was too late in winter for the children to do the feeding when they came from school, so I borrowed one of their bikes, got a large sack to which I sewed two bits of webbing as shoulder straps and stuffed the hay into that. People smiled as I cycled along the Dundonald Road with my sack on my back, and when I took it off I found the sack had said in large print "Prime Sow Weaner".

With all these difficulties increasing around us it became obvious that the ponies would have to be sold. In any case, Barbara was almost too big for Dick and A-levels were beginning to loom up ahead of Anne. And so that chapter of our lives came regretfully to be closed.

29

But if one chapter of our lives closed with the departure of the ponies, another one opened almost at once. Richmond Lodge belonged to the Association of Internationally-Minded Schools and arranged holiday exchanges. Anne and Susan soon found themselves spending a month with a French or German family, and in return the foreign visitors stayed with us. Soon lasting friendships were formed, and now Anne's children exchange with the children of girls who were with us. We were even able to work Barbara into the scheme as well.

At times our house was empty, but when they all came back again we were full to bursting. I thought it might be nice to go for a week's camping in Donegal and combine with some of the girls' school friends who also had exchanges. We raised two cars, two ridge tents and someone loaned us a Continental type tent, which when erected looked more like a young caravan than a tent. It may have been efficient in the wind-still regions of the Mediterranean, but was no match for the Atlantic breezes of Ballyliffen. Unfortunately the owners had lost the instructions about erecting it, so everyone had their own ideas and started screwing metal rods into each other, which looked as if they would conform to some sort of shape, but would then suddenly take a turn in the wrong direction. We laughed so much, we were reduced to almost helpless hysteria, before we got that tent put together and up, and even then it remained a source of distrust. The wind shattered it so much, it shook loose the little metal pins round its base, and next morning I cooked bacon and eggs for twelve on a Primus with one of the French girls beside me to catch the pins before they hopped into the frying pan.

I had chosen Ballyliffen in Inishowen, because I had seen the wonderful three mile long strand of Pollan Bay with the Atlantic breakers rolling in, entirely empty of people, and I thought it would be nice to camp in the sand dunes within sound of the roaring surf. It was, but it also had its drawbacks and I soon realised why it was empty. To begin with, as any sensible camper would know, the sandy soil of sand dunes does not hold the tent pegs, even the big wooden ones, very securely; there is not much in the way of kindling (daily we combed the tide mark for driftwood) and the water had to be fetched by car from Ballyliffen. Catering also was not easy. Bread could only be had from the only shop in Ballyliffen if ordered previously, and when I went into Carndonagh, hoping to buy us some chops, the only thing on offer was three oxtails. However, we all survived somehow, although the visitors must have missed the meals they were accustomed to. The bathing was superb - they never even asked about the temperature, but one day I suggested as a diversion that we should take the cars round Trabeaga Bay and walk up to Hell's Hole on the tip of Malin Head. As we passed the hotel in Malin village I said I thought we should have high tea there that evening, and that quickly circulated amongst the campers as Mrs. Rudnitzky's brightest idea to date.

Long before you reach the edge of the cliff blobs of foam come whizzing towards you, whipped up by the wind, and when you look down, the sea far below is swirling, boiling and foaming round a jagged pinnacle of rock. A truly terrifying place. Far out in the Atlantic it was obvious that a big blow was gathering itself.

By now we had been joined by the boy from next door at home and his school friend, who were doing a cycle tour round Donegal. They had an American bivouac tent, which was made like a big sleeping bag, probably intended for only one soldier, into which they inserted themselves feet first. One of the boys had already caught a chill in his tummy with the attendant embarrassments, and so, after our evening meal which everybody had enjoyed, I asked the proprietor if he had a room for the boy. They were booked out. I explained the situation and wondered if he would allow the boys to spend the night in the lounge within range of the gents.

"They can, surely", he said at once, "but it's a wild night for the rest of you lying out in tents".

I rather thought so too.

"I haven't a place I could put you. I could let you have the ballroom".

I thanked him and accepted it.

So, leaving the boys, we dashed back to camp and bundled all the sleeping bags and belongings into the cars and as the first big drops began to fall, we simply took down the Continental monstrosity. I thought otherwise it would not be in the district by morning.

The hotel had had a lucky fire some years before and had spent the insurance money on adding a ballroom on the top floor. Hopefully this was only used in winter and not when the summer guests were trying to sleep.

As we toiled up the stairs, some of the residents came too and watched us as we unrolled our sleeping bags on the bare floor. "It's going to be hard, mind you", they said. It was.

By now the wind was howling and the rain lashing the windows of the ballroom. "If it's like this tomorrow, we're going home", I said. But when the morning came, Donegal had once again revealed itself in all its sparkling sunlit glory.

The proprietor was very attentive at breakfast. "And are these all your own family?" he asked. Just how he thought one woman could be the mother of fourteen teenagers is beyond my imagination, yet in a country where birth control and abortion are prohibited and where people attest that they have seen statues move, I suppose almost anything is credible.

That kindly man would not accept a penny for his ballroom.

30

Gardeners, like maids, were becoming an endangered species, at least the ones who knew something about gardening, but we were frequently visited by men offering to "redd the place up for ye". We knew from bitter experience not to let them loose unsupervised. But we had a large garden and although Oskar worked hard we needed help. Urgently.

One morning a young man called. I found that, as usual, he did not know much about gardening, but he said he could dig, and so I explained that I was busy in the house that morning, but if he would leave me his address I would drop him a card saying when it would suit me to have him. He was a pleasant looking boy with Edwardian side burns then becoming fashionable with Teddyboys and was wearing a corduroy cloth cap which suited the shape of his head very nicely. As I talked to him I should like to have sketched him, but thought if I asked him to sit that would lead to many complications and possible misunderstandings. He seemed to speak with an English accent from somewhere about the Midlands.

"Are you English or Irish?" I asked.

"Oh, I'm Irish, but I've been over working in England this last year or so."

When I had decided on a suitable day to have him, I wrote him a card, but then I thought, instead of waiting for an answer, it would be better to go to his house and get the answer. He lived in Dundonald.

Unfortunately there was no one in; the state of the front garden did nothing to recommend him as a gardener, however, I popped my card through the letter box, and on the appointed day awaited his arrival.

During the war I had persuaded my father that we should divide our house. At first he was most reluctant "taking in lodgers" as he put it, but I pointed out that with Campbell College being a military hospital, the medical staff were combing the district for digs, and our house could divide very easily making both households independent, apart from sharing the stairs. And after he died, Oskar and I had no compunction about having a tenant as we found the little extra very useful.

On this particular morning as I kept looking out for my gardener our tenant was an elderly lady from Vienna.

"I'm expecting a gardener", I explained, "at least I hope he is a gardener and not a burglar".

"Oh, Honor, you don't really think he might be a burglar".

"Well, I'm satisfied he's no gardener, but he said, he could dig."

"You really ought to be careful."

I agreed. But how was the vegetable garden going to get dug?

To our tenant's relief and, in a way, mine too, he never came. His address stood cocked up on the mantelpiece for some time, until I threw it away in disgust. "I don't know why they bother you about work, if they don't come and take it when it's offered".

Barbara had settled quite happily in Drogheda. We found that if we set off early enough on a Sunday morning, we could be in time for church in Drogheda and wink at Bar across the aisle. We then took her out to lunch in a little pub in Slane where they served an excellent lunch, boiled chicken and ham, I remember it yet, for a very reasonable price. After that we explored New Grange and the other prehistoric relics of the Boyne valley, which have recently been spruced up out of all recognition to the mysterious mounds that we clambered into. Now it is all fenced off and you have to get a ticket.

Returning from such a trip one evening in February, we noticed a pale blue bicycle with ram's horn handlebars propped up against the chestnut tree outside our gate. In the autumn it would have suggested there were boys after the apples, but in the dark at this time of the year it seemed odd, and as we unloaded ourselves at the front door, I saw the curtains in the sun-parlour move and realised the window was open.

"Don't go in", I shouted to Oskar, but already he had opened the front door and a draught screen, which had been placed across it, fell with a crash in the hall. At the same moment a man in a raincoat dashed out of the sunparlour, right across the headlights, and disappeared into the shrubbery. Quickly I attempted to turn the car. "Hop in" I said to everybody.

"I've rung the police", said Oskar, "somebody'd better stay". So he stayed. We only discovered afterwards that a second burglar at that moment was jumping out of the dining-room window on the other side of the house.

Meantime, as we shot down the drive, I set up a real hullaballoo: "Stop that man, he's a burglar. Stop thief. Stop thief". Afterwards the children were amused, "There was no one to hear you, Mum". "Well, there might have been and it would have put them in the picture".

The pale blue bicycle had vanished and Knockdene Park had resumed its empty Sunday night's silence. We swept up to the right and into Green Road. "We've missed him. He couldn't have got this length in the time". So we turned round and went down into King's Road where we saw a couple pushing a pram.

"Have you seen a man on a pale blue bicycle?" I called to them. They obviously thought I was daft and hurried on. "Well, we might as well go home and see what he's taken", said I, preparing to turn into Knockdene Park, when into the headlights glided a young man in a raincoat on a pale blue bicycle. "Quick, Anne", I said, "into Towel House and dial 999. Give them the number of our car and tell them I'll stick on his tail till they come".

There then followed the most extraordinary procession. The burglar rode quite slowly, just as if he were out to take the evening air, and twice waved me up to pass him, finally turning round to know what I wanted.

"I want you to come to the police and I'd be obliged if you came quietly", I said, after which he began to ride faster.

"Mum, you were awfully polite", said Susan afterwards.

"Well, dear, I've never really addressed a burglar before. It's better to begin politely - you can always get rude later."

It was a drizzly evening, and as we passed Cabin Hill Park, a man with his umbrella up appeared.

"Stop that man. He's a burglar", I shouted to him. He could easily have done so, we were crawling uphill so slowly. Instead he stood rigid under his umbrella and watched us pass as if we were a royal procession. On the brow of the hill a van overtook us, and again I shouted to them, but they sped on and turned toward Gilnahirk. Back in Towel House the police had asked if we were heading towards Gilnahirk and Anne had said yes. She was not to know that the burglar would take the other fork towards Dundonald.

So we proceeded at cycle pace along the Old Dundonald Road. A handkerchief was flapping out of the pocket of the raincoat and I wondered if my jewellry, such as it is, was wrapped inside. At Gortin Park he turned left. On either side I could see the flickering light of T.V. sets as their owners tried to squeeze a thrill out of the programmes; if only they would look out of their windows, they might get a real thrill. Crossing South Sperrin our cyclist began to ride in a most peculiar way, zig-zagging from side to side and showing how he could ride without hands. The road went to the right, not having been built on beyond that point, but at the last minute he whipped round down to the left, through a gap and on to the railway line. We followed bumping and banging behind.

"Mum", said Susan, "what's going to happen when we get to the place where the culvert's down?" (Through the ponies' activities we knew every inch of that old railway line.)

"If he doesn't know it's down, he's going to break his neck, but I'm sure he knows".

About a hundred yards short of that place we let Cognac out of the car and he, fully enjoying the chase, streaked away in full cry. Then he and the burglar swept to the right out of the headlights and down the embankment. I stopped the car. I new we had lost him, but I still thought we could frighten him a bit, so I called "Over here, Sergeant, he's down there in the bushes with the light" (the light was quickly turned off) "the man with the dog after him is a burglar".

"Mum, the dog's behind you", whispered Susan. Cognac had evidently been kicked and had retired.

With the cemetery on one side and a cabbage field on the other it might in time have occurred to the burglar that I had only been talking to myself and he might have felt brave enough to come back up the embankment and do something about us. So sadly we withdrew.

As we emerged on to the Old Dundonald Road there suddenly appeared a police car.

"Are you in connection with the burglary in Knockdene Park?" I asked.

"Yes", they said.

"Follow me. I'll show you where he is", I said.

So we sped along the road and swept into the yard of the farm where we used to keep the ponies.

The door was opened by the daughter of the house, but I could hear her mother's enquiring voice in the background.

"It's Mrs. Rudnitzky", answered the girl.

"Are the ponies out again?"

"No, she says it's a burglar she's after and he's down in our cabbage field".

That mobilised the entire family. As they struggled into wellies and seized torches and sticks, I explained where the burglar had last been seen, and then they and three of the policemen vanished into the night. The fourth sat in the police car.

"There is a lane further on, where he might try to come up, if you could just come with us", I suggested.

"I can't leave the car", he said. Quite right. So Susan and I drove off and turned into the lane. Half-way down we saw a flickering light coming towards us, at which point my nerve broke.

"God, here he comes now", I said.

"It's all right, Mum, that's a policeman", said Susan and, thank heavens, it was.

We then saw sporadic flashes as hedges and ditches all round the cabbage field were probed, but the burglar had long since left the district.

Back home there were lights on in every room in the house and the police seemed to be everywhere, but so far as could be seen nothing had been taken. It was assumed that the burglars had arrived just before we did.

Eventually we locked up and prepared for bed, although no one felt able to sleep. We decided all to sleep in our bedroom and the girls dragged their mattresses in to sleep on the floor. We sleep on divans with detachable ends and just when at last we were all settled and almost asleep the end of my bed fell off with a crash that would have wakened the dead.

The next day we had the detectives dusting for fingerprints and producing photos and records. Most of the photos were of men much older than the young man we had chased, but it had meantime occurred to me that where the supposed gardener lived was just on the other side of the railway line from where we had lost the burglar. I described the boy who had called for work to the detectives. One photo bore a resemblance, although the side-burns were gone.

"Do any of these gentlemen live in Moat View Park?" I said.

"Yes".

"This one?"

"Yes".

"I think that looks like the young fellow who came about gardening".

"But it says here, he's working in Leicester".

"Well, does that not tie up with the Midlands English accent?"

At which the two detectives looked at each other and one was kind enough to say: "I think this lady should have our job". They then wanted to be shown the exact route of the chase and were duly amazed at how long we had stuck on his tail. "If anybody deserved to get their man, you did", they said.

"Just as well, we didn't", I said, "I don't know what we would have done with him, I hadn't worked that part of it out".

They called at the house in Dundonald, but were satisfied that the young man with the police record was working in England. So, after all this excitement I had merely identified a young chap who had a police record, but there was nothing to prove that he was our burglar. Still, it was quite a good tale and one, like the Egyptian Princess, that I think we used to get asked out on. I always hoped that in the sign language of burglars our gate posts might have borne a sign saying: Dangerous lunatics - Keep out!

31

Miss Maxwell thought it would be pleasanter for the young French assistante to live for a month in the homes of various pupils, and so she came to us. She got on well with our girls and we asked her if she would like to spend the Easter holidays with us as well, which she did. Her name rather aptly was France - France Diot.

Once again an expedition was planned (with the mother of fourteen teenagers) to climb the Grey Man's Path on Fair Head, and by now some of the older brothers of the teenagers had passed their driving test, so we were able to proceed in three cars.

It was a brilliant April morning, the sea sparkling and Scotland ridiculously near and clear, but there was a treacherous little edge to the wind that suggested rain was not far away.

We left the cars at the farm half-way down the road to Murlough Bay and the party precipitated itself to the foot of the cliff. There with whoops of delight they started to work off their youthful exuberance by leap-frogging amongst the enormous boulders, sometimes dropping down out of sight between the rocks, only to re-appear further on. I remembered at school in Folkestone when we were allowed to bathe in the sea we used to bamboozle the mistress in charge, who was trying to count heads, by duck-diving and staying down as long as possible. I found myself counting heads and I soon realised that it was some time since I had seen France's head popping up. So I called a halt and a roll-call and found, true enough, France was no longer with us.

I told the rest to go on, not to wait for us, as I thought the weather would not last, but to take great care when climbing the path, and I went back to look for France.

I found her sitting forlornly on the stoney shore between two huge rocks.

"I need not have studied so much, if I am to die here", she said.

"Nobody's going to die here", I said rather crossly.

"Oh, I do not mind to die, if only it is QUEECK".

"Come on, give me your hand", and I jerked her to her feet. So, hand in hand we struggled on.

I had discovered that by keeping close into the base of the cliff the going was much easier, in fact from time to time there was the semblance of a path and all that assault-course business with the rocks was not necessary.

"We go up?" asked France at the foot of the Grey Man's Path.

"We go up". I said.

It is not one of those climbs up a sheer rock face where you have to cling on by your eyelids. It is a path formed by a fault in the cliff face, which after centuries has become silted up so that tufts of grass grow on it, and even the odd stunted bush.

"You go first and keep looking up - don't look down", and gripping her ankles I placed each foot firmly on a well-trodden bit of path.

When we reached the top, we were met with a blast of horizontal rain as the first of a number of vicious squalls swept over the moors. The others had reached the cars before the rain came and from all sides sweaters were offered to France, the rest of her we rolled up in the car's rug. I had brought some extra things for myself and soon we were both as warm as toast as we headed for home.

Oskar went through a phase of wanting to photograph ancient Celtic crosses, and now that the family could be left we sometimes set off for several days on such expeditions. Someone lent us a book about the crosses in Inishowen and one Sunday morning we tried to find one which the book said was in the churchyard of a ruined church somewhere near Culdaff. We could see in the middle of a field the ruins of a small building whose gables were much too high for an Irish cottage and which was surrounded by a low wall, but we failed to find any way of getting to it. We hesitated beside a not very promising lane.

The people were coming out of chapel nearby and as two youths approached, Oskar said: "Excuse me, could you tell me if there's a carved cross in there?"

"You couldn't take a car down there", said the first.

"No", said Oskar, "I meant was there a carved cross in there?"

"Ah not at all", said the other, "she's a nice quiet animal".

Feeling the onset of giggles, I withdrew, but Oskar battled on.

"Is it tourists, you are ?" enquired a jovial lady, entering the conversation, her eye on Oskar's camera. "Aye, surely there's a cross beside the old church. That's my field and you're very welcome any time at all to come and take your photos."

So we slithered down the muddy lane and out across the field, but when we reached the wall and looked over, the whole place was waist-high in nettles, and we admitted defeat. However, we felt that we could tell the owner of the book that we had shown willing.

32

I had never taken much interest in politics, in fact I found the whole procedure rather boring. The Northern Ireland politicians squabbled with each other up in Stormont and every Twelfth of July they put on Orange sashes and marched to "the Field", where with vehement rhetoric they avowed their loyalty, although it would appear that not many people listened. Not that I ever was present, but subsequently in photos which appeared in the press some showed family parties enjoying a day in the open and others exhausted Orangemen who had fallen asleep amongst their drums. As a child I hated those big Lambeg drums, which we could hear on summer evenings even in Knock, being paraded "for practice" through the streets of Ballymacarrett. There was no music with them, just the appalling din of several drums together, which the drummers stolidly beat until the blisters on their hands broke and the blood ran down the drumsticks. And sometimes by a change in the wind it seemed they were coming nearer, and I would pull the bedclothes over my ears. No one could explain what it was all about, except that it was part of "the Twelfth".

When Capt. O'Neill, our Prime Minister, invited Mr. Lemass, Eire's Prime Minister, to visit him at Stormont, I was dumbfounded at the furore which that occasioned. Why on earth should not the heads of two neighbouring states meet together for a friendly chat? I simply could not imagine why anyone should object. But then I did not know much about our politicians.

And when Capt. O'Neill opened Corrymeela, the holiday hostel for both our communities to meet together to promote reconciliation, I thought we had a Prime Minister who was worth having.

Shortly afterwards a letter appeared in the Belfast Telegraph from someone who stated that he was a Roman Catholic and how much he appreciated O'Neill's gesture. I did too, and also that this person had had the guts to come out and say so. Not wanting to blossom into print, I wrote to him privately, as he had given his address, thanking him and adding that I thought the time had come for all men of good will to make their voices heard. I was astonished when the Belfast Telegraph rang up asking for permission to print my letter. How they had got hold of it I have no idea, unless the man I wrote to was on their staff. Anyhow, I agreed and the girl said "Under your own name?"

"Of course", I said, "an anonymous letter isn't worth the paper it is written on."

So my letter appeared, and at once I received two tracts, both postmarked Ballymoney, advising me what I must do to be saved. I read them carefully, trying to work out why they had been sent to me: for daring to write appreciatively to a Roman Catholic, or for saying that all men of good will must make their voices heard? I even read out some of the more ridiculous bits to Oskar, but the only conclusion we reached was that there must be some very odd people in Ballymoney.

33

By 1966 both Anne and Susan were at Trinity and as Barbara was due to go to the College of Art, we felt that the time had come to move to a smaller house and garden and that it was no longer necessary for us to live in Belfast. I was born in that house and our three children had grown up in it. I had loved it and its rose garden, yet when 1 came to leave it I felt no regret. The fields where as a child I used to stalk the corncrake had now become Cabin Hill Park and the little old school at Tullycarnet where, as I read Great Expectations, I used to imagine Pip went to school, had been replaced by an enormous school on the other side of the road. As we finally drove away along the Old Dundonald Road, I looked at an incongruous block of flats that was rising and said "Yes, I think it's time we left".

We had grown tired of Ocean Spark's incurable leak. As a family picnic-boat she had fulfilled her role, but now we wanted a bigger boat with a cabin, which did not need the efforts of the entire family to keep afloat. We settled for a Folkboat which would be built in Ramelton in Donegal, and this involved going for a week-end to Rathmullan once a month to supervise progress. The hotel in those days stayed open during the winter, although often we were the only people in it. Eventually at about the time we moved to Lisbane our beautiful new boat was delivered to us and we christened her "Aspidistra".

34

Oskar and I frequently went down to Dublin for concerts in Trinity, the girls both sang in various choirs, and once as a very special favour 0skar was allowed to play in the orchestra for Brahms' Requiem. We always stayed with Millicent, now the sole survivor of that memorable tea-party, rumoured to be about eighty and remaining so for many years, and sometimes we took her to the concert. As we scuttled across Trinity's painful cobbles, we once took her by the arm, one on each side, but she turned and said: "What are you doing to me? You're treating me like an old lady". Once, after enquiring about her health, I said "and are you still driving your car?" "I am", she said, "but I don't like that 'still'." She extricated an elderly vehicle from a narrow little garage, round several awkward corners and then took her friends for drives, "but the trouble with my friends is - they're all so **old**."

Eventually the old lady (although dear help you, if you had so called her) had to go into the Adelaide hospital for an operation and Susan went to visit her. A brash young doctor came round to pep her up and said "and your teeth are your own?" "Yes", she snapped, and after he had gone, she said: "Of course, they're my own. I paid for them. None of his business anyway".

We also went to a series of concerts called "Music in Great Irish Houses" and I remember lovely summer evenings enjoying the Tortellier family playing in the Pompeian decorated ballroom of Castletown House, under its fantastic chandeliers.

One year one of the concerts was held in Clandeboye. The programme stated that a gentleman, whose name I did not know, had sponsored the concert, and as I looked round the room, there was only one gentleman in a dinner jacket, so I thought that must be he. The ladies were wearing a most astonishing collection of garments, some were wafting around in long kaftans, others in what used to be called beach pajamas, but these were in glittering lurex materials, and one lady had baggy Turkish trousers complete with toe-turned-up slippers. Who they were or why they should be dressed like this, I had no idea.

During the interval we adjourned for a glass of wine in a neighbouring room and the elegant gentleman in the dinner jacket began to circulate among the audience. We met old friends of ours, Alec and Muriel (Muriel unfortunately now very deaf) almost at the same moment as I became aware of the elegant gentleman on my other side enquiring how we were enjoying the concert.

"Very much", I said, "and I'm particularly looking forward to the Schubert Trio in the second half".

Alec was saying: "Did you ever see anything like the way some of the ladies are dressed?"

Out of the corner of my mouth I said: "Never seen so many freaks in all my life".

Alec laughed and at once Muriel asked: "What did Honor say?"

"She's never seen so many freaks in all her life."

"What?"

"F-r-e-a-k-s! F=R=E=A=K=S!!"

Oddly enough, the elegant gentleman was still in the vicinity, asking if we had been to any other concerts down South.

I was telling him how much we had enjoyed our visits to Castletown, but Alec was saying: "Honestly, you'd think some of them had come in their pajamas and nighties".

From the corner of my mouth I said: "I think some of them have."

Alec laughed and at once Muriel asked: "What did Honor say?" (etc. see above).

The elegant gentleman had moved on.

Not long after this we went across to Scotland for a few days at the Edinburgh Festival. The Amadeus Quartet gave a really lovely performance of the Schubert Quintet with William Pleeth as the extra cello, which we both enjoyed. After we came home Oskar became very thoughtful and pondered long over the score. He used to play this music himself and he always felt there was something very peculiar about the ending of the Scherzo. The music built itself up into a triumphant climax, broke off for a rest of several beats and then turned back to an earlier passage which was rather lame compared to the triumphant end that was heard just before. Schubert's original manuscript had disappeared, so there was no means of discovering what his intention had been.

After much thought Oskar wrote a letter to the music journal "The Strad", suggesting that the repeat sign had been misplaced. It should be before the climactic build-up, the music should repeat the "lamer" passage and then lead on to the triumphant climax which would then be the end of the movement.

From all sides came letters of agreement, from professional and amateur players, including one from Sir Yehudi Menuhln and from John Reed, the foremost authority on Schubert. Many said that they had always felt unhappy with the ending and now at last Oskar had put his finger on the trouble. Our friend Heinz Hamerschlag had photo-copies made of Oskar's letter and began posting them off to quartets far and wide, all over Europe. The Amadeus replied that they had played it as published for so long, but although they agreed with the new idea they did not want to get involved in musicological arguments. We listened intently any time it was broadcast, some players did and some did not, but for a few short weeks after his letter appeared, I felt Oskar had placed Lisbane on the musical map of the world and was immensely proud.

35

Early in 1969 we went to a concert of the British Music Society in the Whitla Hall at Queen's, but in the interval it was not music that was being discussed. Everyone was gravely concerned about the political situation. It was felt that the Unionist Party was not giving O'Neill the support he deserved. Some thought more people should join the Party in order to support him, others that what was needed was a loyal opposition party; it was much regretted that the only opposition that faced the Unionists wanted a United Ireland, and that prevented many dissatisfied unionists from voting for it. And then a rumour spread around that some of the younger members of the almost defunct Liberal Party were thinking of holding a meeting to discuss the situation and possibly form a 'moderate' reforming movement, to which we said "Let us know if that happens".

In due course we were informed of a meeting in the Wellington Park Hotel, but on the Sunday before that happened, I remember I was just taking the Sunday joint out of the oven when I heard Paisley on the "World at One".

"Honestly, did you hear that awful man?" I asked my astonished family. "All that bullying and bawling, he sounds just like Hitler", and I landed the joint on the table in a fury.

Then and there I wrote a letter to the Belfast Telegraph, in which I referred to him as "this turbulent priest", hoping perhaps that someone would carry out Henry II's request. I also likened him to Hitler, but hoped people would not think he was so absurd as to be not worth bothering about. The letter appeared on the same night as the meeting, and at once the telephone rang. An unknown gentleman, who evidently thought from my name that I was Jewish, began very politely explaining to me how all his uncles and his cousins had fought in the last war and how he had great sympathy with the Jews, but I was wrong on two points in my letter: The Rev Paisley was not a priest - a priest worships a wafer god (which I found a curious statement) - and he is not at all like Hitler.

"He has the same intolerance of people who disagree with him."

"The Rev. Paisley is a man of God".

"But not a man of Peace".

"Christ said: 'I have come not to bring peace, but a sword'."

Now, that is an awkward one, which I would like to hear answered by someone better qualified than I.

"He incites people to hatred", I said. "Have you ever listened to him?"

"I am a member of the Rev. Paisley's church".

"Well, then I have nothing further to say to you", and I put the phone down.

It rang a few minutes later. This time he was not so polite.

"It's a pity you didn't stay in Germany or wherever you come from".

I have since been told by people who have experienced such calls that it is much better to leave the phone off the hook and let them talk to themselves. However, I cost him two calls.

As we went into the meeting a fellow Arellian congratulated me on my letter. "It's time somebody said it", she said.

The meeting proposed that a political movement should be formed to promote moderate opinions and should be called 'The New Ulster Movement'.

Its aims were:

1) To take all possible steps to promote a united community in N. Ireland, based on equality and justice for all.
2) To oppose extremism and establish U.K. standards of democracy in N. Ireland.
3) To call on all people in N. Ireland, who wish to create this new and progressive Ulster within the U.K., to take an active part in political life.

Brian Walker, an Englishman, was elected chairman, with Brian McGuigan, a well-known Belfast solicitor, as vice-chairman. An executive committee was being elected, and I was surprised that the audience seemed to know each other, whilst I, never having been to a political meeting before, knew no one. Then someone said: "I think we should have some ladies". Two were elected and then my Arellian friend said: "I propose Mrs. Honor Rudnitzky", and I was a member of the Executive of N.U.M., something that was to keep me sane during the next two years, when the whole world that I knew seemed to fall apart.

O'Neill declared an election almost the next day after the N.U.M. inaugural meeting, whilst we were enrolling members, but by sending our principles to the prospective candidates we decided to support those Unionists who accepted them. Some returned our information unopened. We received shoals of anonymous letters accusing us of being 'Fenian lovers'. "Do you want to put us into Eire?- We are THE PEOPLE, the Protestant People", but from the more educated populace we received support.

I felt quite inadequate to go out canvassing, so I volunteered to help out in the office. As the weary canvassers returned, relating tales of previous experiences when canvassing for the Liberal Party, my mouth dropped open.

"But I thought the Unionist Party was a respectable party - I mean I knew they were a bit stick-in-the-mud with all that old hat 'Not an Inch' stuff, but I never thought they would behave like that".

"You'll learn", they said.

On election day I thought that I might help as a driver, if I worked with a knocker-up, but was then dispatched to the lower Falls without a knocker-up and found that I had to be a canvasser as well. The people were all very polite, but were always waiting for someone, the plumber, the coalman, a man to fix the back window (it will be the Angel Gabriel, before any of them decide to vote, I thought).

Meantime my brother Morris was faring quite differently. He had had the luck to meet his driver in the war, who volunteered to be his knocker-up and who then rounded up all his friends and relatives with the words "Here's the Colonel come to take you to the Polling Station". None bothered about the Angel Gabriel.

By lunchtime I had delivered one nurse to the Polling Station in Broadway, just outside the hospital complex, and as she said she was going on duty, I think she was glad of the lift. But there was one woman who said she would come out when her husband came home at 3 o'clock, so at 3 o'clock I was there.

It was a raw, miserable February day and when I brought her back, she said: "Would you like a wee cup of tea?"

Ignoring all warnings, I said: "I'd love a wee cup of tea". I enjoyed the crack with her and her husband, we had some good laughs about

Aspidistra looking like a Noah's Ark

Sailing Aspidistra with Susan

In Bunbeg Co. Donegal

Paisley, and when I came out, a youth was hovering. "My Granny would go with you", he said.

The woman whose hospitality I had accepted was evidently a person of importance in that street. Was it possible I had cracked the ice?

"Splendid", I said, would any of her friends like to come too?"

"I'll see", he said, and, becoming my knocker-up, though not as compelling as Morris', he fetched a few more. I hope they all voted for the N.U.M.-approved candidates. When we could entice no more, I thanked him for his help and asked him if he would like to come sailing some day in the summer. "Where to?" he asked doubtfully, apparently fearing he was about to be shanghaied by this strange woman who had appeared in his street.

"On Strangford", I said, "we have a boat. Give me your address and I'll let you know when we have her in the water. Would your brother (who had been taking an interest in the conversation) like to come too?"

So later, on a lovely sunny Saturday, our daughters and their friends, now late teenagers, enjoyed a day's sailing with the two boys from the lower Falls. Fortunately the wind was light and we were able to disperse ourselves on the cabin top and along the deck, so that Aspidistra looked like a Noah's Ark.

36

The New Ulster Movement set about holding meetings all over the Province, at which Brian Walker and others spoke and enrolled members. If we had been sufficiently well organised to have formed a political party I think we would have done well, when a few months later the Cameron Report on the causes of the unrest in 1969 was published. It was highly critical of the Unionist Party. As it was, shocked and scandalised unionists (with a small u) rushed to join us, and for several days I volunteered to help in the office with the flood of enrolments. Afterwards a Quaker friend told another friend of mine: "You know, that morning when I went into the N.U.M. office, I wasn't very sure about them. I'd had a certain sympathy with the Civil Rights people, but then they seemed to be just a front for Sinn Fein, and I didn't want to be taken for a ride. But when I saw Honor sitting there enrolling people, I thought if she is one of them, they must be all right". So far as

I know that is the only benefit I ever was to N.U.M., because as regards politics I was absolutely green and never opened my mouth at meetings. However, I continued to write letters to the Press which always had Brian Walker's approval.

As our membership grew, so too did the volume of hostile anonymous letters. 'We are the PEOPLE. The PROTESTANT PEOPLE' over and over again. Brian was informed that he would be assassinated and the rest of us liquidated, and he wrote to all on the Executive, saying he would quite understand if anyone wished to resign. No one did. I took the precaution of telling the postman: "If a parcel comes for me and it's ticking, would you mind just leaving it down in the garage".

"You expecting a bomb?"

"It said, I was to be liquidated."

"Sounds a bit wet to me".

Some days later, when I was weeding in the front garden, he said: "Well, I'm glad to see you're still ticking over".

"Yes, and I'm glad I seem to be the only thing that's ticking over round here".

By now Oskar had ceased to be a schoolmaster and become a businessman. Two refugees, both former lawyers, had come to Belfast to start a small factory making watch straps. Then one of them died and the other asked Oskar to join the firm, which he did with relief. Most boys do not like learning Latin, and the job of teaching them is a thankless task. He took over the travelling abroad, mostly in the Scandinavian countries, and was often away for weeks at a time.

We lived in a bungalow whose garden divided itself into front and back with two gates on each side of the house. We put stout wooden doors with bolts on those gates, so that now the only easily accessible windows were those in the front of the house, and when alone, I slept much better.

Brian's wife Nancy, however, was worried by the threats. In their case they had their six school-age children in the house, and he phoned me to say he had to go to Paris on business and would I spend a night with his family in Hillsborough. When I arrived, the first thing I saw was a large fire extinguisher in the hall. In spite of having been a leading fireman in the war I had no idea how to work the thing, but I read the instructions carefully, before I went to bed.

Next morning Nancy had a phone call from a distressed N.U.M.

member in Ballynahinch. She was a Roman Catholic and her family had been jeered at coming from school, so I called in there on my way home. Later that family left for England. It is a shame that so many decent Ulstermen and women have left, but where young children are concerned, it is probably the only thing to do.

37

The Provos had their headquarters in Kevin Street in Dublin, and the New Ulster Movement in conjunction with the Irish Labour Party decided to picket them with placards for peace. Susan, who by this time had graduated and was doing her Dip.Ed. in Worcester, happened to be home that week-end and came too. We took up our positions on opposite sides of the street on the corner of Kevin Street, whilst a member from Dungannon stood at the third corner. A lone Garda had been detached to be there, but he, being a man, took up his stance beside the only male member of the trio. Conor Cruise O'Brien came along and shook us all by the hand.

The passers-by were all very friendly and wished me well. Some shook my hand. "It's time somebody's doin' somethin'. It's terrible what's goin' on up there in the North."

"You too could help down here", I said, but that was brushed aside as a comic idea.

I was outside a pub the lower half of whose windows were frosted. Every now and then noses would rise above the frosted glass, like goldfish coming up for air, and I knew I was being observed. Presently a natty sportsjacket issued forth and several noses rose above the glass.

"And what right have you to come down here preaching peace to us?"

"Don't you think everyone should work for peace?"

"You should go back and do it in your own country", and, satisfied that he had put 'that woman' in her place he took himself off.

Then I was surrounded by four excited youths with Northern accents and 'Support the I.R.A.' stickers in their buttonholes. They all spoke at once, reeling off a lot of questions without waiting for the answers, so the discussion became hopelessly confused, and then the one that seemed to be the ringleader said: "Aw come on, she's no good - she doesn't talk right".

I thought I had been doing quite well - at least I gave as good as I got. Only afterwards I learned that it had been rumoured that women from Ballymurphy - who had demanded that the I.R.A. get off their backs - were taking part in the picket, and evidently my accent did not sound right. It is the first time ever that I found a middle class accent an advantage.

Meantime Susan had a woman who said: "You chose a rum spot for your demo. Did you not know the Provos were in Kevin Street?"

Vainly I still wrote letters to the Belfast Telegraph trying to rally "the silent majority" to make their voices heard against the extremists. There was a great deal of apathy, of not wanting to get involved, and I feared that this dumbness might be mistaken for concurrence. Paisley frequently claimed to represent the Protestant people of Ulster and I knew that simply was not true, but not many people bothered to say so openly. Yet any suggestion of reconciliation between our two communities met with wads of anonymous letters signed "True Protestant" or "Loyalist", which became known in the family as Mum's File of Vile Bile. I still have them. They were written on the back page of a note book which had been in the owner's pocket for rather a long time and reminded me of the letters I used to have to wade through in the Censor's Office, and they nearly all arrived on a Tuesday morning, which made me think that somewhere there was a little clique who met together on a Sunday evening after some so-called religious service to decide what liberal opinions ought to be silenced. They frequently told me to go back to Riga as I knew nothing about things here. Why Riga? Then I thought they had all been seamen when Belfast had had a flourishing timber trade with Riga and that was the only foreign part that they knew. Fortunately they were all anonymous, which saved me the bother of answering them, especially the one that said "You Fenian bitch shut your fuckin' mouth". I might not have used moderate language to that one.

But one woman wrote with an address, saying that it was all very well for people who lived in nice safe areas like Lisbane to encourage people to speak out, but I would think differently, if I lived in Ballybeen. I thought she might be worth a visit.

She lived in one of the flats whose access is by a long external corridor. We had a free and friendly chat. She disagreed with the bully boys who she said were everywhere in the estate, but thought that the only thing to do was to keep your head down and say nothing. I could see what she meant, for as we talked shadows were continually flitting across her window blind, and if you had been at all outspoken, a petrol bomb could so easily have come through the glass.

The New Ulster Movement was holding a meeting in Tullycarnet Leisure Centre the next week and I told her she would not feel so isolated, if she went to it, but she never came. Perhaps she was frightened someone from the estate might see her going in. Fear is the means by which the bullyboys keep their grip on the masses, just as it was in Germany under the Nazis.

38

The New Ulster Movement continued to hold meetings in all parts of the Province, but the people who came to them were the "converts" and if we wanted to test what support we had from a wider public, we realised that we would have to become a political party. Brian Walker always counselled patience, to wait until we had sufficient support and above all more money and then to time the launch to some moment of crisis. It was a thousand pities that we had not been properly organised at the time when the Cameron Report published its criticism of the Unionist Party.

Although I do not think I contributed to the discussion, I listened intently to the arguments put forward, the how and when and why. I remember Oliver Napier saying: "Well, it may fall flat on its face, but could you live with yourself, if you didn't try?" His words were something that subsequently I found most comforting, when support for Alliance in Comber seemed hard to raise - at least it let me live with myself, and when I was suddenly asked to say something at our 21st birthday party in 1991, I reminded him of what he had said. It was manifest that the Party had not fallen on its face and that after 21 years it was very much alive and kicking.

Just before our elections I heard someone on the radio being questioned about his involvement with Alliance and what it stood for. He replied that it was a party which supported the link with Britain and at the same time wished to promote friendly relations with Eire. At once I said that was not why I joined Alliance.

I set out my views and the "Alliance News" printed them. "Of course, I want to support the British link and have friendly relations with Eire, but the main reason I joined was because I wanted to heal the divisions in our society. Until we do that there will never be peace. I wanted the minority to feel that Stormont was their parliament in which they were fairly represented, not 'a Protestant parliament for a Protestant people'. I wanted to see the end of religious discrimination in jobs and housing and to encourage the welding together of our young people through integrated education".

Well, at the end of 21 years we have not achieved all of these things, although progress has been made. Yet I am as certain that they are the only hope for our future as I was the day I joined Alliance.

But back to 1970 when the Alliance Party was born.

The Stormont parliament had been prorogued and we were due to elect a fresh Assembly in June, based on Proportional Representation, but before that could take place the Local Government Elections, also based on P.R., were scheduled for May 1973.

An Alliance member came down to see me and to ask, if I would stand as the local candidate in the Comber area. My immediate reaction was "No thanks. Not my cup of tea. I have no interest in local politics and I would make a hopeless councillor, because I always think what I might have said on the way home".

"You seem well able to express yourself in your letters".

"Maybe. I always have my best ideas in the bath, which makes it impossible. Besides, I couldn't be bothered catting and fighting about who should be awarded the contract (on religious grounds) for doing this or that. I couldn't care less, if they were heathen Chinese, so long as they did the job properly", and I bundled him off.

But then, a few days later, Paisley made one of his outrageous statements and as usual no one said a word. No Unionist would dare, because it would cost them votes from their own hard-liners, and I thought "For Pete's sake, why doesn't somebody do something?" A little quiet voice within me said "Well, you were asked and you said 'not my cup of tea', so after consulting Oskar, who was very supportive, I rang up and said "All right."

Thus I embarked on a new phase, not that I had any illusions about being capable of dealing with that monster Bully Boy, but at least my votes might help to swell Alliance's total.

39

Over the years I had come to realise that nursery schools were not only of tremendous benefit to the children, but in Northern Ireland they were specially so. They opened their doors to the neighbourhood without bothering about which community the children belonged to. The toddlers similarly accepted each other as playmates, and through the monthly mothers' meetings the mothers were welded together by their common interest in their children's well-being. When the Peace Line was erected, some mothers found themselves cut off, but they braved the jeers and taunts of their own faction by continuing to bring their children through the barricade. One mother was heard to remark in astonishment: "I never knew she was one of 'them'" to be countered by another "Well, I don't care what she is; she's a decent wee woman anyway". Alas, those remarks belong to the era of *Once Upon a Time.*

In 1973 the Nursery School Association celebrated its Golden Jubilee in London. I had kept up my interest in nursery schools and, having served on various management committees and become chairman of the Belfast Branch, by now I was chairman of the N. Ireland area of the Association and as such was invited to attend the celebrations in London. We were invited by our president, Mrs.Renee Short M.P., to take tea the previous afternoon in the House of Commons. It sounded like the sort of occasion that called for a posh hat, so I borrowed one from Nancy.

Kathleen McCormack, a fellow Arellian, who had played such a tremendous part in the setting up of the Arellian Nursery School, the first in all Ireland, and subsequently had never ceased to further the nursery school movement, was also invited. At first she hesitated. She was no longer young and her eyesight was not so good. Barbara was working as a receptionist in a hotel in London and I suggested to Kathleen that if she stayed there, Bar would be at hand to look after her; and this was arranged.

Bar had a bed-sit in Clapham, where I intended to stay. The house belonged to a doctor who ran his surgery in the basement, and there were two other tenants, another girl, and at the top of the house an elderly man who was convinced that the two young girls could not be relied upon to lock up properly when they left in the mornings.

Tea in the House of Commons was interesting, although, the weather being overcast and chilly for May, it did not take place on the terrace, as

I had hoped it might. Perhaps we were too large a group.

Bar left at an early hour the next morning and later, but in good time to pick up Kathleen from the hotel, I attempted to follow her. But try as I might, I could not get the front door open. At last, in desperation, I rang Bar.

"Oh, hell", she said, "it's that silly old duffer upstairs. He's double-locked it".

"Where's the key?"

"In my handbag here".

"What on earth am I going to do?"

"How good are you at mountaineering?"

"Not bad. But I'm not really dressed for that sort of thing."

"Listen, Mum. Go out of the back door - mind you snib it behind you - and get up on the coal bunker and from there you can get on to the garage roof and drop down at the front of the house".

"Tell Miss McCormack what's happened. Get her a taxi and tell her to go on. I'll follow her, if I can."

"I'll tell her you are on your way", said Bar, and I fancied she was grinning.

As the snib of the back door clicked shut behind me, I thought, "if I don't make it over the roof, I'm now stuck here for the rest of the day".

The best way for Nancy's hat to travel was on my head, so I put it on and addressed myself to the coal bunker. It proved to be a rather unstable structure, so I passed on quickly to the flat garage roof, which also creaked a bit. I decided not to stand up but to try to distribute my weight, so pushing my case before me I proceeded on all fours, hoping that my nylons would be equal to it. I noticed a man on the far side of the railway line observing me with interest. This is going to look good in print, I thought, "Native of N. Ireland apprehended while behaving in a suspicious manner on a roof in Clapham". When I reached the far side of the roof, I was appalled to find there was a twelve foot drop into the forecourt. Between it and the basement steps there was a flat-topped balustrade which might be reached by rolling on to my tummy and feeling for it with my foot. But if I missed, I could end up very much lower at the bottom of the basement.

Just then a man came out of the surgery.

"I wonder, could you help me?" I said.

Without a word he took my case and set it down.

"If you could just guide my foot on to the wall", I said, rolling over and hoping that he wasn't seeing more than he should. He grasped both my feet and placed them firmly on the balustrade, from where the rest was easy.

I thanked him profusely and still without uttering a single word he took himself off. Whether he was dumb or whether he assisted ladies down off roofs every day of the week will never be known. Anyhow, I was not hanging about until the man from across the railway came round with a policeman. Seizing my case, I sprinted the length of Claxton Grove and hopped on a bus.

I had long admired Kathleen as a level-headed pragmatist, but never more so than on that morning. Bar had explained the situation to her, and whereas many another elderly lady might have been flustered, "put out" as they say, Kathleen took it all in her stride and swept my apologies aside.

The ceremony had begun, when we reached the hall, but officials swooped on their important guest and, pinning a flower on her bosom, wafted her away to the vacant seat on the platform, whilst I sank thankfully into oblivion on a seat at the back.

When I again focussed on the proceedings, I found that our president who was Labour, and the Minister for Education, Mrs. Margaret Thatcher who was Conservative, were exchanging pointed but guarded remarks; but as it was a convivial, celebratory occasion, both ladies kept their claws well sheathed. The Minister assured us all that her Ministry would do all that it possibly could do to further nursery education and, as I say, since it was a well-mannered festivity, no-one upped and said: "We'll believe that when we see it".

40

Back home again, I turned my attention to the local elections.

I had never placed much confidence in the efficacy of canvassing. I dis1ike being cajoled on the doorstep into buying something which I do not particularly want, be it soap powder, toothbrushes or Jehovah's Witness's literature, and usually close the door saying "Nothing to-day, thank you". But if I was to stand for election, and not many people in Comber new me, I supposed I would have to go through with it, although I could not believe that my appearing on their doorstep would make people instantly give me their vote.

A member from a neighbouring branch had offered to help in Comber, where we never had enough canvassers and, hearing that he was very good at the job, I attached myself to him to see how it should be done. Also it made it easier, if he made the introduction.

In a backstreet the door was opened by a rather dim young woman.

"Good evening", said Hugh, "we've called on behalf of the Alliance Party."

The young woman continued to look at us - dimly.

"You've heard of the Alliance Party, haven't you? said Hugh, faltering slightly.

"Is that the Inurance?"

When we had enlightened her, she recollected that she had seen it on T.V., "but you know, we just turn it off. We're not interested".

I went home to Oskar and said: "Here we are teetering towards the edge of the abyss, from which, if England gives us the boot, there will be no return, and people just aren't interested."

An older woman said: "My husband always voted Unionist".

"Could we have a word with your husband?"

"He's dead these eight years. But I wouldn't like to go against his wishes".

"You just can't win", growled Hugh as we came away.

After that he had to return to his own branch and I found myself going it alone.

I could write another book about the answers you get.

"Oh dear, no, we don't vote. We're Christian" (that is not peculiar to Comber, it occurs elsewhere).

"Aye, I know all that. But still, I wouldn't like NOT to vote Unionist".

"Well, dear, I'm for King Billy and the pipe bands."

A man swaggered over to me and said: "I seen one of your Alliance candidates had a very queer name", in the what-have-you-to-say-to-that? tone of voice.

"Like Rudnitzky?" I asked.

"Aye, sumpin like that."

"That's me".

I have seldom seen a man more dropped on. I think he was one of those people who enjoy confiding to their friends that they 'know for a fact' and what he knew for a fact about Alliance was that it was hand in glove with the Communist Party. But I shattered his idea of a K.G.B. agent.

The candidate .....

..... with Caramel as guardian

One evening the door was opened by a youngish man who said: "Ah, good evening, Mrs.Rudnitzky". This was a pleasant change; someone who knew me by name. "No, I'm sorry you won't be getting my vote. I've promised that to the Vanguard man". (Vanguard was an extreme Protestant organisation with militant tendencies.) "Him and me was at school together, but the wife here says she'll vote for you".

A young woman with a baby in her arms appeared. A few weeks previously I had been talking to the Young Wives in Comber about nursery schools, and I thought this was probably one of the Young Wives.

"My Daddy and my Mammy say they're going to vote for you. You remember my Daddy, don't you? He was the steward at the club out at Whiterock".

I thanked them and as I withdrew, the husband said: "I'm sorry about that now. But maybe in the next election I'll vote Alliance for the Assembly".

I walked away thinking what kind of mixed-up kids do we have in Comber. How can anyone vote for Vanguard in one election and Alliance in the next? Like children playing oranges and lemons, they bestow their favours first on one side and then the other, so that no one need be offended.

In the end, to my relief, I was not elected, but my first preference votes, when transferred to my running mate, got him elected, which was a satisfactory conclusion.

Someone who studied the results said to me in disbelief afterwards: "Did you know two of your first preference votes transferred to Vanguard?"

I said: "I have an idea how that happened".

As I said earlier, the way votes are won in elections has nothing whatever to do with political ideologies.

41

We enjoyed sailing our new boat, *Aspidistra*. It had a cabin, two decent berths and two for pygmies in the bow, a cooker and a toilet, so that we could entertain friends on board who were not very used to sailing. There were four other Folk Boats and an attempt was made to race us as a class, but it never really got going and instead we just raced in the handicap class at the regattas.

The first fibre glass boat, a beautiful-looking cruiser, had appeared on Strangford - now, of course, everything is fibre glass, even dinghies -and after the race in Portaferry we were all ashore in the hotel and the topic was fibre glass.

I said: "Well, I'm old-fashioned. I think if a fibre glass boat was hit really hard, it might just crack open like an eggshell".

It was a lovely summer evening, but by the time we set out for home the wind had dropped and we put on the engine. When under sail, I steered, but once the engine was on, I left it all to Oskar and took as little as possible to do with that engine and its tantrums. I went below and got supper which we ate in the cockpit, watching the seals and the cormorants, with the sunset slowly spreading over the sky and Scrabo pricking up in the distance.

The anchorage in Whiterock Bay was becoming very crowded so, armed with the boathook, I went up on deck in good time to pick up the mooring. I thought Oskar was coming in rather fast and signalled him to slow down, but we roared on. I made a frenzied stab and hooked up the mooring, but shouted that I could not hold it and let it fly again. When I looked back, Oskar had disappeared. He was on the floor of the cockpit, engaged in a death grapple with the gear lever. And suddenly, dead ahead, was the beautiful fibre glass boat which, if we continued, we ought to hit just about amidships. I bellowed so loudly, I wonder people did not hear me at the crossroads, and just in the nick of time Oskar grabbed the helm again and disaster was averted. We only came to rest when he took the key out of the ignition. I never really trusted that engine again.

Neither of us knew much, or indeed anything, about navigation and sadly we had left it rather late in life to learn. We new our way round Strangford and its many islands, the passage between them at certain tides, and, by personal contact, we knew many of its pladdies, but the Irish Sea was quite unknown to us. We made several trips to the Isle of Man by simply keeping our eyes on it until we got there. Once when thick fog descended on us, Oskar found it by the Radio Direction Finder, which pleased him greatly and amazed me. I had resigned myself to seeing the dawn coming up over the Welsh mountains. And the next day, the fog still sitting like a thick blanket between us and home, he found Ireland again, although of course that was easier, being harder to miss. But we emerged from the fog almost at the point of the coast of Co. Down, where Oskar thought we ought to be, which further amazed me.

Once with Susan we set out for Scotland, but Oskar was not well and the weather being dull and unpleasant, although July, and visibility murky, we put into Donaghadee and rang up Anne to take us home. The next day we returned the boat to Whiterock and instead set off in the car for an unplanned 'take-pot-luck' holiday in Donegal and Sligo, which was less fraught with anxieties. Eventually Susan accompanied by two Swiss friends, who had sailed in the Mediterranean and had passed exams in seamanship in the thorough-going way that the Swiss do, did manage to make Scotland, but her parents never ventured again. Instead we enjoyed several years of making day-trips on Strangford, with an occasional race at the regattas.

However, as time went on we became ruefully aware of the advantages of fibre glass. Anne was married and rearing a young family near Ballygowan, Susan was teaching in an International School in Zurich, and Barbara was pursuing a variety of jobs in England, where she eventually married. Thus every spring it fell to the parents to get the boat ready: scraping, sand-papering and varnishing, and that decided us it was time to sell.

So regretfully another chapter of our lives closed, but almost at once another one opened.

42

Susan had acquired a small car, and for several Easters she drove us round Switzerland, northern Italy, Burgundy, the Loire and once we even went as far as Provence and along the Mediterranean coast. She knows her way around, when to make use of the motorways to hurry through less interesting parts and when to leave them and shoot off up some quite impossible-looking mountain-track to see some unique little church or village. She even found places to park in Florence and Sienna, which was quite something.

She and her Swiss friend had rooms in an old house at the lakeside which belonged to a fisherman. He and his wife lived on the ground floor with Susan and Marianne above, and Marianne very kindly went home to her parents for Easter and allowed us to use her room. The

Breakfast with Susan in Switzerland

In Fürberg near Salzburg

With three of our four granddaughters

Oskar still enjoys his quartet

fisherman set his nets in the evening and then very early in the morning went out to lift them, and at about 7 a.m. we would hear the put-put of his engine coming back over the still waters of the lake. All the cats of the neighbourhood could be seen strolling nonchalantly in single file down the garden path, tails held stiffly erect in pleasurable anticipation.

Else had long since left us as our Nanny and had married. Her husband had business connections with Malta, which he visited several times a year and where they had a house. We spent several pleasant holidays with them on that ancient and interesting island. One evening at supper with Maltese friends I remarked how picturesque it was away from the developed parts and the giant hotels and regretted that I had not brought my paint box. At once the lady of the house said she had given her husband a box of oil paints for Christmas, which he had never used, and pressed them upon me.

Anyone who has ever lived in Malta will know what I mean about church bells on feast days. Every tiny hamlet has its chapel and every chapel has its bell, often emitting no more than a rather tinny jangle, but determined to outdo its neighbouring rival. At the first gleam of dawn some little faraway bell begins to tinkle, to be joined at once by its indignant rival, hurrying to catch up; then some of the larger churches join in with bigger, deeper, full-throated boomers, and soon they are all at it, and further sleep is impossible. I got up and looked out of the window. In the backyard some scrawny cats were scavenging round the bins - not a very picturesque subject - so I dressed and went up to the market place. There, although it was not yet six all was bustle and commotion.

Two empty packing cases stood nearby and, sitting on one, I set up my canvas on the other. Presently a little man appeared, wanting something. From under his cap his little brown monkey's eyes made beseech and he laid his hands on the packing cases. I indicated that, of course, he could have them but at once we were surrounded by people all apparently on my side and scolding the poor little man. These were then burst aside by the cafe-proprietor, who with a flourish set down two chairs.

"For you, madam", he said, adding, "I make you plenty room", and with a further flourish of his arms did so.

But the onlookers, like chickens evicted from an Irish cottage, soon returned, furtively at first, but eventually pressing round me. They watched my every movement, following my brush from palette to canvas, rubber-necking like a Wimbledon crowd. I found their presence irksome.

The Maltese wear a great deal of black. The men wore black trousers with white shirts and either black or white cloth caps, but the women were dressed almost entirely in black. Some wore the Faldetta, a curious headdress, which I suppose must be attached to their shoulders and which then arches up in a stiffened canopy over the head, but not resting on it. All in black, of course, with a black veil down the back.

The market stalls were colourful enough in the brilliant sunshine under the dark tamarisk trees, but I soon grew tired of painting so many black figures, and as a majestic lady sauntered past us I gave her a yellow blouse. A little gasp rippled through my audience. No respected matron would ever be seen in the market place in a yellow blouse.

For a few moments the priest breathed heavily beside me. He had a rounded brow and his beads rocked to and fro like the painter of an idle dinghy.

By now the sun was beginning to get hot; I was not satisfied with my painting and disliked painting in public and so, gathering my things together, I bowed my gratitude to the distant cafe-owner and set off for breakfast, trying to keep ahead of the children without actually running. But one little boy pursued me persistently and when at length I turned to chase him off, with a very sweet smile he handed me my glasses.

43

Back home again we soon became absorbed in the developing political situation. An Assembly had been elected to Stormont. It was our first attempt at power-sharing between our divided community and I honestly believe that if only it had been allowed to continue we might in time have achieved peace, and it would not have been necessary for Mrs. Thatcher to make another attempt with the Anglo-Irish Agreement. But because the subsequent Sunningdale Agreement allowed the Eire government to be included in a consultative capacity the extreme loyalists were opposed to it, although Paisley and his party took their seats in the Assembly.

Mass protest rallies were held, which in May 1974 became much more serious with the threat of an all-out strike. At first it was referred to as the "loyalists' strike", but as it soon became too ridiculous that "loyalists" should be defying the British government, it became known as the "Workers' Strike". Not that all workers supported it. Many who would have gone to work were prevented by the road blocks set up by the strikers, who also seemed to control the supply of electricity, so that those who managed to reach their place of work had to be sent home.

Oskar and Else had a sister, Lotte, who had survived the war in Germany and in 1974 she decided to come and visit them both. It was arranged that she should go to Else and husband first and when they went off to Malta she should come to us, but that coincided with the time that Oskar would be in Scandinavia on business. It was one of those things that might have been arranged differently with a little better communication. Not that I minded coping with Lotte on my own. She had stayed with us before, her English was good and my German passable, but almost at once the so-called Loyalist Workers' Strike began to brew up, and it became difficult to take her around to entertain her.

It was very difficult to find out what was happening and I felt very isolated and frustrated. No one seemed to be doing anything against the strikers, but just before Lotte came to stay I heard that Len Murray, the leader of the T.U.C. was coming over to lead a march of workers back to Shorts and decided I would try to help that. So, early in the morning I took the car and picked up some men who were thumbing a lift at Dundonald and delivered them to the assembly point and went back for some more near Ballyhackamore. A futile gesture, maybe, but it eased my feelings. The march went off at halfcock; it was not well attended.

After that I became absorbed in the day to day problems of existing. We cook by Calor, so there was no problem there, at least until the drum was empty, but the supply of electricity was so unreliable, there never seemed to be enough hot water for a bath.

The first target of the strikers seemed to be transport and the electricity supply. Road blocks were set up everywhere preventing people from getting to work or anywhere else, and the electricity went on and off unpredictably. Sometimes there were news bulletins or news flashes on the radio and sometimes on TV. Every time Merlyn Rees appeared, he looked more distraught than he did before, until I thought the poor man would have a nervous breakdown. Everyone seemed to be standing back waiting for everyone else to make a move to face the strikers. It was impossible to get a paper, the Belfast Telegraph was blacked, and it was very difficult to find out what was happening, much less to explain it all to Lotte. She was astonished one morning to find me doing the ironing at six a.m. (as I had done the washing the previous morning at that time, because I had discovered electricity was on then).

"Why do they not pay the workers and settle the thing?" she said.

"It's not that sort of a strike", I said, "they want to bring down the government."

"But then it is not a strike at all", she said, "it is an uprising."

"You could call it that."

"Why don't they bring in the army?" said Lotte, doubtless thinking that that is what would be done in Germany.

"There is a great danger of civil war and no one wants to provoke that."

As things got more chaotic each day, I became really worried and suggested to Lotte that she should go home whilst she still could.

It really was the craziest time I have ever lived through. Daily there came the most horrendous reports from the power stations that there was only so many hours' supply left and then the sewage pumps would break down and the streets of Belfast would be flooded with sewage. It was impossible to know how it would all end or when.

I was not sure that I could get Lotte up to Aldergrove with all the road blocks or that I would even have enough petrol. Then one evening from a darkened and apparently closed wayside filling station a car switched on its light and drew out, and I guessed it might have been getting petrol.

"Could you give me some?" I asked the man.

"Turn out your lights", he said, "I could let you have two gallons." And there in total darkness we both stood, listening intently. In any normal country we were not doing anything wrong, yet here in our own native land we feared to be caught in this simple transaction.

Strangely enough, Lotte had no difficulty in getting through on the 'phone to the airport and her daughter in Frankfurt. I had found it impossible to phone Belfast, but "vital services" they said were being maintained.

I had worked out how to get to Aldergrove without going through Belfast and hopefully avoiding most of the road blocks. A big question mark hung over the crossing of the main Ballynahinch road at Temple, it was always daubed with forbidding loyalist graffiti, but as we drew near I was relieved to see an army vehicle parked in a nearby lane. The crossing was deserted.

The last comment on the strike we shall leave to Lotte. She had hoped to call into Bell's for some coffee beans on our way to the airport as good coffee was still rare in Germany, but when I counselled against it, pointing out that there were already three known road blocks between us and Belfast and that we should try to go round by Lisburn, she looked at me.

"But this is like it was under the Nazis".

So I said good-bye to Lotte, and on my way home saw an astonishing scene in Saintfield, where a lorry with calor gas cylinders was besieged by a mob, all trying to buy a cylinder off it before it got any further. I was a blood donor and was due at St. Mary's church hall that afternoon, but when I reached Comber I found cars, two abreast, circling the square with the police regulating them. Kane's evidently had petrol.

I explained to a policeman that as a blood donor I wanted to get through into the church, and then said "What's all this? Is it only for loyalists and their pals?"

"Not at all", he said, "it's for everybody. And we are here to see you get it. Two gallons each."

"But I'd never get in."

"I'll get you in", he said, and after I had got it and again circled the square, he got me into the church car park.

I gave off to the girl who was looking after me my views on the strike and the strikers, and when she had done, I said "Now that's a decent drop of Alliance blood. See and stick it into some of these kyhoots". (That was a lovely word of my mother's that I have never heard anyone else use, but it expressed my feelings exactly.)

"I thought it must be", she smiled, "I am a member myself, but of course we can't discuss politics, when we are on duty". She then gave me VIP treatment, carrying all my belongings over to the rest bay and bringing me a cup of tea.

"You made my day", she said.

Well, it was nice to know that anyway.

As I rose after my brief rest, I saw the policeman stretched out on the next-door bed. So that was it. Favouritism from one blood donor to another

With Lotte safely on her way home I felt relieved of some of my worries and took the dog for our favourite walk up Scrogy Lane. It was a lovely evening and the Lough with all its islands looked so peaceful, it was hard to imagine all the distressing things that were happening, all the bitterness and hatred that came so easily to the surface.

As I came down again a neighbour was working in his front garden. "Have you heard the news? The government's fallen."

"Oh my goodness, that's terrible."

"Why do you say that?" he asked in some surprise.

"Because it will be so much easier for the British to ditch us."

"Oh no, Mrs.Rudnitzky, they'll not do that. Not after all we did for them in two world wars."

"They won't ditch us as long as the IRA keep on attacking us. But if the loyalists start to defy them too, well, I mean, why should they bother any more? There's plenty of people over there who would be happy to be rid of us".

We disagreed and parted.

Alone in the house that night I felt very sad. The Sunningdale Agreement had raised so many hopes of peace. I wondered if the "Loyalists" really knew what they had done. I remembered three young girls being interviewed about why they had come out on strike.

"They come in and told us we had to get out", said one.

"They said we had to show Workers' Solidarity", said another.

"But why, what about?

A pause. "It's about Sunningdale", said the third.

"And what is Sunningdale?"

None of them knew.

And when Oskar eventually came back, he was equally bewildered and dismayed. Everywhere the strikers were jubilant. From our front door we looked across the peaceful Lough to where two columns of smoke were spiralling into the evening air above Newtownards.

"What's happening there?" said Oskar.

"Victory bonfires, probably."

"Funeral pyres," he said.

However, it was not the end of the world; we were not ignominiously booted out of the United Kingdom as I had feared we might have been and tales soon circulated of personal experiences. Anne's had not been happy. She was teaching in Rupert Stanley College and got through the barricade by explaining that she had students shortly to sit exams and she wanted to give them their last lessons, only to find, when she arrived, that the college was closing, because so few people had managed to get there. On the way back the strikers were more truculent and started to bounce and rock the car so that she thought they were going to overturn it with her inside. Desperately she pleaded that she had a two-month old baby (my first grand-daughter) waiting for her at home and they let her go.

But not all tales were so ugly. There was the lady, a staunch Orangewoman, who was perturbed to learn that the strikers had commandeered Comber's Orange Hall from where they were issuing permits for petrol. She went along to investigate and found some of Comber's lay-abouts sitting at a table.

"And who do you think you are?" she said.

"The Workers."

"The W O R K E R S", she screamed, "there's not one of you has done a hand's turn from the day you left school. Well, seeing I'm here you might as well write me out one of your wee chits - if you can write that is."

Laboriously, tongue protruding, one of them penned out a ticket.

She had no car, neither could she even drive, but I hope she got a good price for her permit.

And the Alliance member who was stopped on her way to work in Newtownards. Ahead of her were half a dozen cars, each driven by one man who, obedient to the bully-boy in charge, turned round and went away. But she stayed where she was, kept her engine running and beckoned the bully-boy to come back to her. When told she could go no further, she said "That's what you think" and put her foot flat on the accelerator. The rest of the road-blockers skipped aside. Sadly, when she reached her office, an architect's office where they worked under neon lights, she found they were being sent home, because there was no electricity.

She said, "I was angry the first time, but now I'd cooled down and didn't relish having to go back through them again."

However, as she approached the strikers, she heard one of them say "Oh Gawd, here's this woman comin' back again," and they all departed.

It is a pity that the Labour Government or the Northern Ireland Office or whoever was supposed to be governing us at that time had not just a wee bit of that woman's guts.

44

In 1977 the Local Government Elections came round again. Again I was asked to stand for Alliance in Comber and again I said "No thanks". I thought it would be so much better if we had a Roman Catholic candidate and I visited several of our members to try to persuade them. But they did not want to stand any more than I did. It seemed that our councillor Jim McBriar would not be re-elected on his own without a running mate whose votes would transfer, so if all that was required was a peg on which to hang a few hundred Alliance votes, I consented.

We were always short of canvassers in the Comber Branch and once again I set off on my own, trying to sell myself and the Alliance principles on the door steps. It was the only time I have ever been chased.

It happened on a country road, where I had stopped the car at a new bungalow, which had neither letter box, bell or knocker. It is quite extraordinary how many houses are like this, particularly in the country; I wonder how the postman manages. Having battered my knuckles on the front door, I decided to go round to the back and as I did so, a young fellow on a tractor flew past. He looked back sharply several times and turned into a field at the bottom of the hill, where a little red Mini was sitting. I thought I'm sure he's wondering what I'm doing prowling round somebody's backyard.

As I came down the hill, he suddenly ran out shouting and waving his arms. At first I thought some animal had broken out and wondered if I could help, but then I caught the word "Alliance" and drove on round the corner. I had just stopped at the next house, when round the corner came the little red Mini, so fast that he had to screech his brakes to stop. It was now obvious that I was the target for his abuse.

I got out of the car and said: "Did you wish to speak to me?" This seemed to floor him. He shuffled off into another field opposite and once safely behind the hedge started up again, something about Alliance which I could not quite hear.

All my Alliance literature lay on the back seat of the car. If I leave the car open, this lunatic may scatter it; if I lock up, he may damage the car. And then I saw Caramel. Normally a very sweet-tempered dog, she was quivering with indignation. She had fixed her eye on him with a sharp glint I had never seen before, and on her neck all her hackles were up. I thought I can safely leave everything to the dog, and I went up the garden path.

The lady of the house had a bell, was in, and, even more surprisingly, was favourable to Alliance. We had quite a chat and then I asked her who farmed the field opposite. She told me and I asked if there were any sons.

"Yes, very nice boys", she said.

"Then it must have been someone who works for them."

"Why?" she asked.

I told her about the young fellow's performance.

"I'll come down with you to the gate and see who it is. That's no way to behave."

He was still dodging about behind the hedge, but she greeted him by name and said to me: "I'll have a word with him". I took the opportunity to depart.

It was only at the next house, as I handed in my leaflet, that I noticed my hand was shaking slightly. It had not been a pleasant experience.

Nor was that the end of it. Next morning there was a battering at the front door. Oskar opened it, but he did not want to speak to Oskar, he wanted me. I said: "If you have anything to say, please do so through your solicitor", and closed the door. But still he kept on shouting something about Alliance, which was difficult to hear, because by this time Caramel was indicating how much she would like to eat him. Getting Oskar to restrain her, I again opened the door and said: "Look, if you don't clear off, I'll have to call the police", but only when he saw me lifting the receiver and pretending to dial, did he do so.

Afterwards I did ring the police. I said I didn't wish any action to be taken, but I thought this young fellow was taking electioneering a bit too seriously and should be told to cool it. Whether the police bothered to do so -I am sure they had many more important things to do - but if they did, it might explain the boy's father's behaviour.

The election had followed the pattern of the previous one. To my relief I was not elected, but with the help of my transferred votes Jim was returned.

So was the boy's father as a good Unionist.

Some days after the first council meeting, Lord Dunleath rang me up to say that a Unionist councillor had complained to him about something I had said about his son during the election campaign. At once I said: "I can tell you exactly what happened".

"I don't want to know", said Henry, "I told him I would have a word

This is where we belong

with you. I've done that now and so far as I am concerned that is the end of the matter".

I quite saw how Henry would not want to become embroiled in petty squabbling, but all the same I thought he might have heard my side of it. Besides I should have been interested to know what I was supposed to have said.

Regrettably my tales of the last twenty years are not very happy ones. From time to time hopes have been raised that some way out of all the bitterness, bloodshed and hatred might be found, only to be dashed. O'Neill once said that Ulster stood at the crossroads, and it seems that we have since taken a wrong turning. There have been many worthy attempts to heal our divisions and undoubtedly Alliance has proved that people can put their differences behind them when working for the good of the country, but in spite of this attitudes have hardened on both sides and violence has escalated. Our politicians sadly seem to be more concerned in a sordid struggle for power than in trying to find a solution, and Mrs. Thatcher's Anglo-Irish Agreement was met with even more resistance than the earlier attempts at a workable settlement had been. Everywhere graffiti appeared defiantly proclaiming "Ulster says No", but that, it seemed, was all that Ulster had to say.

At one time I became so saddened and depressed at the way things were going here that I seriously thought we should leave. In Germany Oskar had waited five years thinking that the Nazis would not be tolerated much longer and that sooner or later the German people would come to their senses. I said "We are not sitting here until the bully boys take over completely".

Barbara and her husband were running a small pub in a picturesque Cotswold village, where we had stayed and felt at home. I asked her if she could find us a nice wee Cotswold cottage somewhere there. She said "They are hard to come by, cost the earth, and anyway are not really suitable for the elderly. They're built of solid stone, all right in summer, but hard to heat in winter and their stairs are always very steep and narrow - they wouldn't suit Daddy's arthritic knees. You'd be better in a modern bungalow". So she went round several house agents who sent us lots of leaflets.

We studied them carefully, neat little houses built in enclaves with nothing to look at but other neat little houses, and when we looked at them and then from our front door looked out over the lovely view we have over Strangford Lough we knew we belonged here, come what may.

And so we just hope and pray that reason will return and that some day people will echo that Nursery School mother of long ago and say of their playmates, school fellows, colleagues or neighbours "I don't care what they are, they're decent people anyway" and our grandchildren, or maybe our great-grandchildren, may one day be able to enjoy the Ulster that we once knew and loved.